Learning and earning

How a value chain learning alliance strengthens
farmer entrepreneurship in Ethiopia

Learning and earning

How a value chain learning alliance strengthens farmer entrepreneurship in Ethiopia

John Belt and Wim Goris
with Sorsa Debela, Firew Kefyalew, Eva Smulders
and Piet Visser

This publication is jointly produced by the Royal Tropical Institute (KIT) under the umbrella of the Agri-ProFocus network in collaboration with Agriterra, Cordaid, FFARM, ICCO, IIRR and SNV.

Agri-ProFocus
PO Box 108, 6800 AC Arnhem, the Netherlands
www.agri-profocus.nl

Agriterra
PO Box 158, 6800 AD Arnhem, the Netherlands
www.agriterra.org

Catholic Organisation for Relief and Development Aid – Cordaid
PO Box 16440, 2500 BK The Hague, the Netherlands
www.cordaid.nl

Facilitating Farmers' Access to Remunerative Markets – FFARM
PO Box 10068, Addis Ababa, Ethiopia

Interchurch Organisation for Development Cooperation – ICCO
PO Box 8190, 3503 RD Utrecht, the Netherlands
www.icco.nl

International Institute of Rural Reconstruction – IIRR
Ethiopia Country Office, PO Box 7931, Addis Ababa, Ethiopia
www.iirr.org

Royal Tropical Institute – KIT
PO Box 95001, 1090 HA Amsterdam, the Netherlands
www.kit.nl

Netherlands Development Organisation – SNV
SNV Ethiopia Country Office, P.O. Box 40675, Addis Ababa, Ethiopia
www.snvworld.org

Contents

Figures

Tables

Boxes

Photos

Foreword

How can we assist smallholders to cope with market challenges and secure market access and better incomes? What strategies can NGOs and business development services adopt to support this type of farmer? How can they create opportunities for the poor, and eliminate bottlenecks for their inclusion in dynamic chains?

These questions are posed in the foreword of the publication *Chain empowerment: supporting African farmers to develop markets* (KIT et al., 2006). We repeat them here, because the idea for the Learning Alliance was born in June 2006, right after the launch of this publication in Ethiopia by KIT and IIRR. We both were present at the first working session of the Alliance in Debre Zeit in March 2007, and we both witnessed the increasing levels of entrepreneurship: farmers and service providers at work, instead of NGOs instructing farmers. Since then, an energetic and out-of-the-box loop of action and reflection on farmer market relations in the Ethiopian Learning Alliance emerged.

For our Ethiopian network of members, partners and producer organizations, it was the first network activity, covering all the aspects of value chain development. This book describes the results and lessons. It focuses on two key areas. First, how can entrepreneurial farmers connect to markets and value chains? Second, what are the basic capacities and competencies required from producer organisations and service providers (NGOs and business development services) to support entrepreneurial farmers?

The conclusion: improving market relations means changing support relations. The successful farmers and NGOs in the Learning Alliance linked up with business partners and research institutes, thereby broadening the support base for farmer entrepreneurship. This pragmatic approach to improve chain relations and performance gives scope to multiplying and up-scaling the approach with a substantial buy-in from private sector actors.

Within the Agri-ProFocus partnership, the Learning Alliance was one of the first joint activities, inspiring later joint action in Rwanda and other focus countries. The partnership adopted the learning-by-doing mentality: the current focus on farmer entrepreneurship and multi-stakeholder "Agri-Hub" centres is about improving skills and relations to find answers on the "how" question above for each specific situation and context.

We would like to emphasize the courage, passion and determination of the team, thinking out of the box in starting new ventures against all odds during the Learning Alliance process. And, last but not least, we would like to thank them for taking time to reflect on lessons learned and to share them in such a respectful and open way with all of us.
So, please find a quiet corner, and enjoy the reading.

Hedwig Bruggeman, director Agri-ProFocus
Rem Neefjes, director SNV Ethiopia

Acknowledgements

Agri-ProFocus and KIT are very grateful to all the farmers, NGO staff, cooperative managers, government officials, bank employees, private-sector players and researchers for sharing their knowledge and experiences to the benefit of the Ethiopia Learning Alliance. They were the key players in the Learning Alliance initiative; they kept its focus relevant and practical.

A special word of gratitude to four people who gave birth to the Learning Alliance idea: Lucian Peppelenbos of KIT, Rem Neefjes of SNV, Isaac Bekalo of IIRR and Egbert Hoving of ICCO. They were the enthusiastic pioneers every innovation needs.

Special thanks to Agriterra, Cordaid, ICCO and DGIS, Netherlands Directorate-General of Development Cooperation for investing funds in this joint endeavour. Also to FFARM, ICCO, IIRR and SNV for allowing their staff members Sorsa Debela, Eva Smulders, Firew Kefyalew and Piet Visser to dedicate a large part of their work to the Learning Alliance. They played a vital role in coordinating the Learning Alliance process in Ethiopia, always keeping a close eye that the Alliance connected to the daily reality of farmers and their organizations.

Finally, many thanks to Paul Mundy (the editor) and to Rozemarijn Apotheker, Ellen Mangnus, Anna Laven, Vera Hendriks and Roel Snelders (proofreaders) for their help in bringing this publication to life.

John Belt and Wim Goris

Abbreviations

ETB   Ethiopian birr. In February 2010, US$ 1 = ETB 12.6 and €1 = ETB 17.5
(ETB 100 = US$ 7.91 = €5.71)
FMO   Farmers' marketing organization
NGO   Non-governmental organization
SNNPR Southern Nations, Nationalities and Peoples Region

Contributors

John Belt (j.belt@kit.nl) is senior advisor in sustainable economic development at
the Royal Tropical Institute (KIT).

Sorsa Debela (buluudoo@yahoo.com) is general manager of FFARM Ethiopia.

Wim Goris (wgoris@agri-profocus.nl) is network facilitator at Agri-ProFocus.

Firew Kefyalew (firew.kefyalew@iirr.org) is national director of the Ethiopia office of IIRR.

Eva Smulders (eva.smulders@iccoenkerkinactie.nl) is Agri-Profocus country coordinator,
Local Market Development Programme Ethiopia, ICCO.

Piet Visser (pvisser@snvworld.org) is senior advisor in economic development for SNV
Ethiopia.

1   From production to marketing to chains

"How can we grow enough to feed our family?"

Growing enough to eat is a problem faced by smallholder farmers all over the developing world, day after day, year after year. The farmers try to produce as much as they can, on small plots of land, with limited inputs, and under threat of drought, floods, pests and diseases. If the harvest fails, the grain store will be empty, and the family will go hungry. If the harvest is good, that gives a good start to the new season.

That is why many farmers' groups and agricultural development organizations also focus on production. They help farmers buy inputs, get better seed, control weeds, keep their crops and animals free of disease, try out new practices and harvest higher yields. Most agricultural research and extension efforts also concentrate on production questions: boosting yields, improving tolerance to pests and diseases, and getting more out of a limited set of resources.

"How can we earn enough to feed our family?"

Production is important, but it is not everything. Production may go up, but costs for seed, fertilizer and labour may also rise, perhaps even to a level where the farmer makes no profit. As production rises, prices tend to fall. Farmers may harvest a bumper crop, but be worse off than before because the price has sunk faster than output has risen. A farmer with a truckload of produce is helpless without a buyer willing to buy it and to pay a decent price, and without a truck on which to load it.

Such considerations have become more important with trade liberalization and globalization. The removal of price controls, the demise of government commodity boards, and the lifting of restrictions on imports have exposed farmers in many countries to the market for the first time. At the same time, greater freedom in choosing what to produce and where to sell it has opened up new options for farmers. Likewise, improvements in roads and other infrastructure have presented new marketing opportunities to many farmers in previously remote areas. So the question for farmers is increasingly, "how can we **earn** enough to feed our family?"

Farmers, their organizations, the NGOs and public agencies that serve them, have to adjust to these new realities. They need to reorient themselves to deal with marketing: to produce what can be sold in profitable way, rather than merely growing as much as possible in the hope that it can be sold. This sounds straightforward, but in practice it appears many organizations and their staff struggle with this new paradigm.

"How can we improve our position in the value chain?"

Most farmers sell part or all of their harvest to a trader. Traders sell the produce to other intermediaries, such as wholesalers or retailers. Food products follow many stages before they reach their final destination, the consumer: the way food travels from "farm to fork" or from "seed to plate" is called a **supply chain** or **value chain** (see Box 1).

Many people and organizations make a living in a value chain, undertaking activities such as bulking, grading, processing, transporting and packaging. Farmers are part of this complex, interdependent commercial system of bringing food to consumers. Any change in this system influences the farmer. For instance, urban consumers may start to prefer bread over maize meal. Farmers come to realize that traders are less interested in maize, buying less and offering lower prices. Another example: supermarkets are on the rise in many developing countries (see Vorley et al. 2007). That puts strong pressure on the traditional retail sector, such as open-air markets, small groceries and butchers, sometimes even putting them out of business. Farmers and traders supplying these traditional retailers will feel the pinch, and they need to find ways to link to supermarkets.

The value chain concept highlights that a farmer is influenced not only by the market he or she sells to, but also by the other stages and transactions that follow in the chain. These stages influence the farmers' market and thereby the price the farmer gets for his or her crop. So apart from reviewing the market they supply directly, farmers also need to look at their position in the wider value chain. Is their position being eroded by changes at the retail or consumer levels? Can they improve their position by switching to alternative crops? Can they improve it by engaging in grading, transporting or processing? How can they make sure that in the long term their farms will generate enough money for their families?

A value chain perspective enables farmers, their organizations, NGOs and public agencies supporting them to look beyond production and marketing at the farm gate. It reviews the wider commercial system the farmers participate in, especially looking at the position farmers have in this system. Their position can only be sustained or improved when the positions of the other chain players such as traders, wholesalers, retailers, consumers are taken into account. A value chain perspective also looks at the implications of longer-term changes in the food system, such as rise of supermarkets, cheap imports, and changing consumption patterns. This perspective is vital if we are interested in improving the lives of farming communities.

New skills needed

Many farmers' organizations and NGOs recognize the need to look beyond production and beyond marketing at the farmer's level. They see the need for a new approach, but find it difficult to make the adjustments required. They need a new mindset, new knowledge, new skills, new staff, and perhaps a new organizational structure. They need

Box 1. The value chain concept

Figure 1 below gives a simplified picture of the value chain concept that was used time and again during the Learning Alliance. In the centre is the **value chain** where different players do different activities to get the product "from farm to fork". The value chain concept stresses that these players depend on each other in an interrelated commercial system. Figure 1 aims to express that what happens at one level influences the other levels in the chain.

Around the value chain are people that provide **services** to the chain players without directly taking part in growing, transforming, trading or consuming the product itself. Typical support services are transporters, banks, extension agents, electricity companies etc. Whether or not these services are available, accessible and of good quality has direct influence on the way the chain players can do their work.

The chain actors and supporters are operating in a wider environment, the **chain context**. This typically involves macro economic issues such as exchange rates, interest rates, governmental policies, legislation and judicial system but also things like climate and infrastructure. These conditions determine how the chain players can operate.

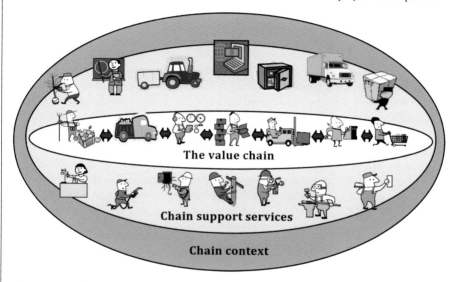

The value chain

Chain support services

Chain context

Figure 1.   The value chain concept

new approaches and skills in business, marketing and finance, as well as the opportunity to explore, learn and adapt them to the specific situations where they work. These skills include the following:

Understanding value chains. To select a product to sell, and to market it effectively, farmers must understand not only their immediate market situation, but also how a complete value chain works. Doing so might open a range of new options for them: use the collected information to negotiate for better prices, find a different buyer, grow a different product, package it in a different way, or process it before selling it. That will enable them to earn more.

Organizing as a group. Few smallholder farmers grow enough of a particular product to sell it effectively. A few sacks do not fill up a truck, so traders must negotiate with many individual farmers in order to get a full load for their vehicle. This means transaction costs become very high. Traders prefer a central place to pick up the load. One answer is for farmers to get organized and sell their produce as a group. That has many advantages: by selling in bulk, the farmers can negotiate for a better price or sell to a more distant market. They can attract traders by offering a central location where all the produce will be assembled. Working as a group also makes it easier to share information and skills, learn about new opportunities, test new approaches or access inputs at a lower price.

But organizing for marketing is not easy at all. Working together can be tough, especially when it involves money: money that is earned only once or twice a year and that needs to cover the family's basic needs for a whole year. It sometimes means coordinating planting and harvesting times, growing one variety, maintaining quality standards, sorting and grading the produce, and packaging. It also means selecting a buyer, negotiating over prices and conditions, and arranging collection and transport. All this requires leadership, organization, mutual trust and a common vision. These qualities are hard to obtain and are easily lost.

Accessing finance and other business services. Successful farming depends on a range of business services: access to inputs, financial services, training, market information, transport, government support schemes, and so on. These services are not always available or may be too expensive for farmers. The providers may have failed to adjust their services to new circumstances and new demands from their clients, for instance by maintaining a production rather than a market focus. The required services are often closed to individual farmers but may be accessible to a group. For example, an extension worker is unlikely to have the time to visit individual farmers, but is happy to work with a well-organized group. A group can establish an internal savings and loans scheme, or may be able to attract a loan from a bank or microcredit institution. On their end, the providers of the services need to be flexible, pro-active and client-oriented to be able to reap the benefits. Their main concern is to offer services that farmers need and can afford.

Business planning. Viewing farming as a business is key in a liberalized market system. Farmers need to be able to analyse their potential markets, identify their potential customers, negotiate successful deals with buyers and input suppliers, work out their costs and expected income, look at their longer term position in the value chain, develop a business plan, and put the plan into operation. A farmer is an entrepreneur, like any other business person.

Empowering farmers in the chain

The Agri-ProFocus partners chose a Learning Alliance methodology to strengthen these skills for a group of 18 Ethiopian farmer organizations and 14 local NGOs supporting them. This approach was in part inspired by the publication *"Chain empowerment"* (KIT et al. 2006), which proposes that small-scale farmers can strengthen their participation in value chains in two ways.

First, farmers can develop activities beyond production, such as procuring inputs, drying, sorting and grading, processing, transporting and trading. Developing these kinds of **chain activities** is known as "vertical integration". It is reflected in the vertical axis in Figure 2.

Second, farmers can develop their influence in decision making and control over the chain. This may include deciding on volume, price conditions, terms of payment, setting grades and standards, targeting new groups of consumers, and triggering innovations. Developing these aspects of **chain management** is known as "horizontal integration". It is shown as the horizontal axis in Figure 2.

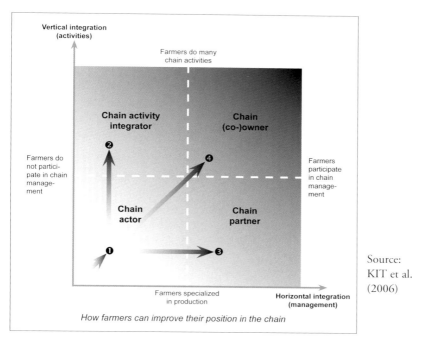

Source: KIT et al. (2006)

Figure 2.   Dimensions of empowering farmers in the value chain

This framework reveals different strategies for empowering farmers in value chains (the numbers refer to Figure 2):

❶ **Upgrading as a chain actor.** The farmers become crop specialists with a clear market orientation.

❷ **Adding value through vertical integration.** The farmers move into joint processing and marketing in order to add value.

❸ **Developing chain partnerships.** The farmers build long-term alliances with buyers that are centred on shared interests and mutual growth.

❹ **Developing ownership over the chain.** The farmers try to build direct linkages with consumer markets.

Which strategy is best depends on the context: the type of product, market conditions (such as level of competition), available financial services, existing technology, the farmers' willingness to collaborate, their business skills, and government policies. The strategy should suit the circumstances. And over time, conditions might change. The last option (developing ownership over the chain, ❹ in Figure 2) is therefore not necessary the best strategy: in some situations it makes more business sense to upgrade as a chain actor (❶), add value (❷), or develop chain partnerships (❸).

For example, most small-scale dairy farmers will not have sufficient production volumes or the required financial resources to build their own dairy plant: they simply can't afford the costly processing equipment. This means the option of vertical integration is blocked since it is not commercially feasible. For these farmers it makes much more sense to improve their productivity (upgrading as a chain actor) or develop linkages with the processing industry (developing chain partnerships). In many Northern countries, farmers focus on becoming better crop specialists and attracting the best buyers from the market place (upgrading as a chain actor), not bothering about adding more chain activities to their work portfolio (adding value through vertical integration) – and some make a good living out of their business. These examples show that chain empowerment strategies are context specific.

This two-dimensional framework was instrumental in designing the Ethiopia Learning Alliance. The four strategies identified were the basis for promoting farmer empowerment in the value chain. Development of the new skills, as mentioned in the previous section, was an integral part of this approach, as was developing knowledge on specific themes which are critical in enhancing farmer entrepreneurship (see Chapter 3).

Agriculture in Ethiopia

The Federal Democratic Republic of Ethiopia is the second-most populous nation in Africa: over 84.9 million people were living in the country in 2010. Ethiopia covers 1.13 million km^2, making it the 10th largest country in Africa. The gross national product per capita was US$ 330 in 2009. Life expectancy at birth is 56 years for men and 59 years for women (sources: UNdata, n.d. and Ethiopian Government Portal, n.d.).

Agriculture is the largest sector of the Ethiopian economy, accounting for 47% of the gross domestic product, 60% of the country's exports, and 80% of its employment. Some 85% of the country's 80 million people depend on cropping or livestock for their livelihoods. Most of these are smallholders with 0.25–1 ha of land. Frequent drought, suboptimal cultivation practices and low levels of investment combine to keep output and productivity low.

Emerging from a period of dictatorship, the country has liberalized much of its agricultural sector. But the marketing of agricultural produce in the country remains weak, despite rising consumer demand as the population and cities grow. Infrastructure is poor, but roads are improving gradually, opening up new opportunities to farmers close by. Value chains are long and fragmented, quality standards are ineffective, and market information is limited. Farmers and their organizations are focused on production, and business services are weak.

Both the government and local and international NGOs promote farmers' organizations as a way to improve opportunities for the country's rural population. According to the Federal Cooperative Agency, some 5 million Ethiopian farmers are members of over 25,000 cooperatives. Around 3,800 of these cooperatives are organized into 174 cooperative unions. Some 2,800 cooperatives are engaged in the production and marketing of grain, coffee, vegetables, dairy products, fish, honey and other products. The government believes there is considerable scope for using existing farmers' organizations as a basis for strengthening the production and marketing of agricultural products in Ethiopia. This ambition is included in the key policy document *Ethiopia's Growth and Transformation Plan* (MoFED, 2010).

The Agri-ProFocus Ethiopia Learning Alliance

The Netherlands has a longstanding relationship with Ethiopia in the area of development cooperation and business relations. Dutch development agencies that support agricultural and rural development in Ethiopia work with a network of national and local partner NGOs and farmer organizations in Ethiopia. These Dutch development agencies are all members of Agri-ProFocus, a networking organization whose objective is to connect and align an array of development, business and knowledge organizations working on rural and agricultural development in Africa, Asia and Latin America.

In 2007 Agri-ProFocus brought together a group of Dutch development agencies working in Ethiopia to explore exchange and collaboration. A shared concern was the need to enhance farmer entrepreneurship and empower farmers in markets and value chains. A number of agencies, including ICCO, Cordaid, SNV, KIT and Agriterra, agreed to work together, along with their Ethiopian partners, to develop a joint programme to do this.

Consultations with their partners gave rise to focus on strengthening business skills of farmers' organizations through a "Learning Alliance" (see Chapter 2 for an explanation of this approach). The Alliance consisted of three types of partners (see Annex 1):

- **Eighteen farmers' organizations** from Amhara, Oromia and the Southern Nations, Nationalities and Peoples (SNNPR) regional states (Figure 3). These organizations were either farmers' marketing organizations (FMOs) or established cooperatives; some were general-purpose, while others focused on a particular commodity such as coffee and gum. They ranged in size from 40 to 900 members, and had a turnover of between ETB 3,500 to 380,000 (US$ 280 to 30,000).

- **Fourteen local NGOs** that were already working with the farmers' organizations on food security and cooperative development. Most of these NGOs were based in Addis Ababa, the Ethiopian capital, and had field offices or representatives in the villages or small towns in Oromia or SNNPR. Some of the NGOs were working with more than one of the 18 farmers' organizations.

- **Eight development organizations**, six from the Netherlands (ICCO, SNV, KIT, Cordaid, Agriterra and Agri-ProFocus), of which two have a local presence in Ethiopia (ICCO and SNV), and two from Ethiopia (IIRR and FFARM) (see Annex 2).

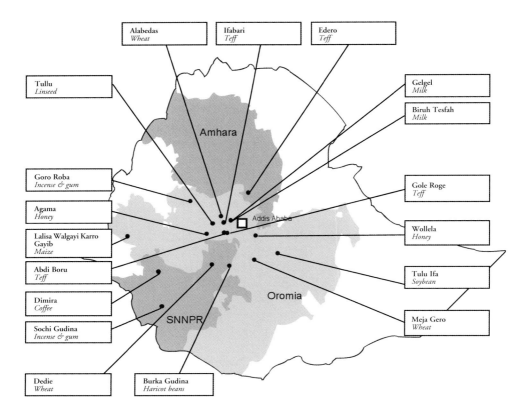

Figure 3.   Farmers' organizations in the Learning Alliance

A support team was formed consisting of one representative from each development organization. This team managed the whole Learning Alliance process. The following roles were played by the different organizations:

- **Coaching**. FFARM, ICCO, IIRR and SNV provided staff who coached the participating farmers' organizations and NGOs to carry out the field assignments that were part of the Learning Alliance process.

- **Funding**. Agriterra, Cordaid and ICCO provided funding to support the Learning Alliance activities.

- **Technical expertise**. KIT provided technical guidance on the Learning Alliance process and took a lead role in developing the field assignments, workshop design and documentation.

- **Coordination**. Agri-ProFocus was responsible for the overall coordination of the Learning Alliance involving communication, budget control and managing the partnership process.

- **Facilitation**. IIRR facilitated the six workshops that were held during the Learning Alliance trajectory.

Set-up of this bulletin

This bulletin is organized in five chapters. The next chapter introduces the main features of the Learning Alliance approach. Chapter three describes in detail the topics covered and type of activities carried out. Chapter four presents the main results of the initiative. The last chapter draws the main lessons and give some recommendations for running a Learning Alliance.

Between each of the chapters are stories of the 18 farmers' organizations and their NGOs. These stories were written by the farmers and NGO staff together, assisted by local journalists. Besides describing some activities and results, the stories illustrate what the farmers learned during the Learning Alliance.

The farmers' stories are clustered along the value chains they deal with, forming five product groups:

- Teff (page 22)

- Wheat and maize (page 37)

- Dairy and coffee (page 65)

- Haricot beans, soybean and linseed (page 77)

- Honey and incense (page 93).

Teff

Linking with research: The Edero Cooperative

Location: Denbi Gerarge, Enesaro woreda, Northern Shoa zone, Amhara state
Founded: 1977/1978
Members: 743 (182 women)
Product: Teff
Supported by: Ethiopian Orthodox Church–Development and InterChurch Aid
                Commission (EOC–DIDAC), and ICCO

A farmers' cooperative that buys teff grain from its members, sells fertilizer, fodder and other items, and offers loans to members.

The Edero Cooperative had unsuccessfully tried to deal with a range of crops. They traded teff, sold fertilizer and fodder to their members. However, these operations suffered from inadequate management, limited market information and a lack of working capital.

Through the Learning Alliance, the cooperative learned that it would be better to concentrate on the marketing of one type of crop. It selected teff, a staple food grain that is in high demand and grows well in the area. Members learned how to produce high-quality teff, and the cooperative timed its sales carefully to boost its profits.

To raise production further, the cooperative started to work with the Debre Zeit Agricultural Research Centre. The researchers provided improved seed, and helped an initial 20 members to test new, promising teff varieties. Results were encouraging: yields nearly doubled from 1.3 to 2.4 tonnes per hectare. The cooperative now plans to distribute the improved varieties to the remaining members.

Triggered by the Learning Alliance, the Edero Cooperative learned how to handle the cooperative's finances in a better way, by improving its book-keeping, careful monitoring income and expenditures, managing financial flows, and working closely with microfinance institutions. The cooperative also improved the financial management of the savings-and-credit association it had established for its members. Now it is looking for expansion in this area: it plans to offer savings-and-credit schemes especially for poor women.

The cooperative's successes in production, marketing and credit services have attracted new members. During the Learning Alliance, membership increased from 665 to 743, further boosting the co-op's financial situation.

A clear focus: Ifabari Farmers' Marketing Organization

Location: Borecho, Dendii woreda, West Shoa zone, Oromia state
Founded: 2000
Members: 372 (71 women)
Product: Teff
Supported by: HUNDEE Oromo Grassroots Development Initiative and ICCO
Business contest: First prize ✳

This farmers' organization buys, stores and sells grains grown by its members and provides financial services.

The overall winner of the business plan competition (see Chapter 3) was the Ifabari Farmers' Marketing Organization (FMO), operating near Ginchii town, some 70 km west of Addis Ababa. In this area farmers are used to growing wheat and teff. Alongside the FMO, Ifabari has established a women's association to help its female members save money. The women began by saving just ETB 0.5 a week, depositing it with the association. The following year, the weekly contribution was raised to ETB 1, and it is now ETB 2. Because they have a savings history, members can now get credit to run small businesses. Ifabari has grown from an initial 67 to 372 members. At harvest time, all members donate 10 kg of teff for poor people in the village to borrow and repay without interest.

During the Learning Alliance activities, Ifabari focused on teff. It learned how to map its markets, strengthened its negotiation abilities, calculated members' production costs, identified major challenges and corresponding solutions, introduced the concept of product quality, and taught members how to increase their productivity and profits. Ifabari and HUNDEE created an alliance with three other FMOs to bulk and sell high-quality teff. They also obtained improved seeds and technical support from the Debre Zeit Agricultural Research Centre to increase productivity and product quality.

Ifabari's business plan outlines how it intends to sell two grades of white teff in markets in Ginchii and in Addis Ababa. To reach this goal it will negotiate orders with three selected wholesalers in Addis Ababa, establish a retail outlet in Ginchii, and contract a transport firm to deliver the teff to its customers.

The jury of the business plan contest awarded Ifabari the first prize because *"Ifabari's business plan stands out in terms of its simplicity and clear direction. The organization maintains focus on its core business (teff selling and marketing), while at the same time improving all chain elements (from input supply to diversifying the market outlet). In addition, the cooperative's representatives showed great passion, enthusiasm and entrepreneurial vision. The jury is convinced that the prize money will give the alliance of Ifabari and three other FMOs another boost to become even more productive, sustainable and profitable."*

Growing confidence to raise productivity:
Abdi Boru Farmers' Marketing Association

Location: Bacho woreda, South West Shoa zone, Oromia state
Founded: 2006
Members: 83 (30 women)
Product: Teff
Supported by: Oromo Self-Reliance Association (OSRA), and ICCO

A marketing association selling teff.

"Creating awareness was the key", says Tesfaye Debebe, secretary of the 83-member Abdi Boru Farmers' Marketing Organization. *"None of us realized that farming was a business"*, he says. The association members picked up technical and organizational skills throughout the Learning Alliance, and that has helped change their attitudes and learn about new opportunities.

Abdi Boru came to existence one year before the Learning Alliance started. Its 18 founding members had contributed ETB 5,000 in working capital. A local NGO loaned it another ETB 9,000.

At the start of the Learning Alliance, the association identified several challenges: limited business understanding and financial resources, low participation by women, and lack of skills in documentation and keeping financial records. It addressed its shortage of financial means by increasing its turnover, selling shares and adding members, thereby boosting its working capital to ETB 86,000. It also established strong linkages with microfinance institutions and trained its members in financial management, both paving the way for accessing loans in the future.

Instead of producing and selling a range of crops, the Abdi Boru association decided to focus on just one: teff. This staple grain is in high demand, and teff grown in Becho enjoys a good reputation among consumers. By improving quality and targeting the market in nearby Addis Ababa, the association aims to more than double its volume to 384 tonnes, and to realize a five times higher profit in three years. Abdi Boru expects that this will enable the association to invest in a mill to grind the grain of members and other local farmers.

A new business orientation:
Gole Roge Farmers' Marketing Service Cooperative Society

Location: Nanno Garbel woreda, South West Shoa zone, Oromia state
Founded: 2005
Members: 107 members (30 women)
Product: Teff
Supported by: Facilitators for Change and ICCO
Business contest: Second prize ❋

An alliance of six farmers' organizations that bulks and markets teff.

Buying grain at harvest time and storing it until the price has gone up sounds like a good business strategy. This approach was followed by the Gole Roge Farmers' Marketing Service Cooperative Society: it used to buy wheat, teff, linseed and other food grains from its members and stored them for a later sale. Such a strategy depends on business skills and good information (especially if prices fluctuate widely), so managers know what to buy and when to sell. But without such skills and information, the Gole Roge cooperative found it had low turnover and was not making profit.

After improving their business skills through the Learning Alliance, the Gole Roge cooperative and its members changed their approach. The farmers started to focus on crops they could sell at a profit, rather than merely selling their surplus. Calculating their costs and income enabled them to know when they were selling at a profit. They began to demand better seed, so the cooperative started producing seed by multiplying improved varieties of teff supplied by the Debre Zeit Agricultural Research Centre. This strategy was successful: in 2010 the cooperative produced 20 tonnes of teff seed for sale to its members. As a result yields have more than doubled to 2.4 tonnes per hectare. At the same time, Gole Roge has arranged with microfinance institutions to provide loans at acceptable interest rates to its members.

The cooperative has also improved its marketing. It has established an alliance with six other farmers' associations so it can better supply the quantities that customers need. It has expanded its customer base, for example by signing agreements to supply teff to staff of the state education bureau and to a consumer association in Addis Ababa.

2   The Learning Alliance approach

A Learning Alliance is a group of organizations that come together to learn how to deal with a particular set of problems, or to learn a specific approach. Typically a mix of organizations participates: NGOs, private sector, government agencies and research institutions. The participants follow a series of steps, each building on the previous one. Each step focuses on practical application and draws on the participants' own experience as well as lessons from elsewhere. It involves peer-to-peer exchange as well as training and coaching.

The process hinges on "learning by doing", following a popular phrase in adult education: "what we hear, we forget; what we see, we remember; what we do, we understand". In other words, the approach is very much rooted in practice.

The Learning Alliance in Ethiopia was inspired by the work of the International Centre for Tropical Agriculture (CIAT) in Central and South America (Lundy et al., 2005; Lundy, 2006; Lundy and Gottret, 2007). CIAT's initiative used a research perspective to develop agro-enterprises, while the Ethiopia Learning Alliance focused on farmers' practice using a value-chain perspective. Nevertheless, several key elements remained the same as CIAT's: developing entrepreneurship, enhancing business orientation of farmer communities, promoting farmers' organizations, and joint learning among a diverse group of stakeholders.

The Ethiopian Learning Alliance covered each of the skills outlined in Chapter 1 (pages 14–16): understanding value chains, organizing as a group, accessing finance and business services, and business planning. Each of these was one "step" on the "ladder" of the Learning Alliance process. Two additional steps were added, one at the beginning (inception), and one at the end (a business contest), making six steps in all (Figure 4):

1. Inception
2. Mapping the chain
3. Strengthening chain actors
4. Financial and business services
5. Business planning
6. Business contest

These steps are described in more detail in the next chapter.

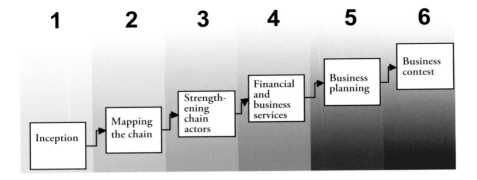

Figure 4.   Six steps in the Learning Alliance process

Four types of activities

Each step consisted of four types of activities:

- An **initial workshop**, during which the topic was introduced.

- An **assignment** to collect information and generate insights into the topic.

- **Coaching** to help the participating organizations fulfil the assignment.

- Presentation of findings during a second, **exchange workshop**. Each organization reported on the results of the assignment, and the participants discussed their experiences.

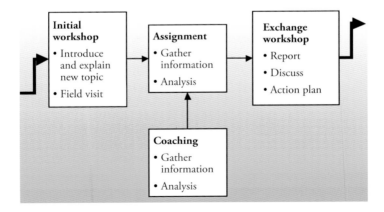

Figure 5.   Activities in each step in the Learning Alliance process

Initial workshop

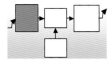

The Learning Alliance support team organized this workshop at a convenient location and time. The workshop lasted 1 or 2 days. Participants included representatives of the farmers' organizations and the support NGOs, along with members of the support team and resource people.

A workshop consisted of three main types of activity:

- **Introduction of new topic**. The support team introduced the topic of the workshop – for example "how to map the value chain" in step 2. Depending on the complexity of the topic, this might include presentations by resource persons, panel discussions, group exercises and games. The aim was not to make the participants experts in the new material, but to introduce it to them and give them a basic understanding of what it was about.

- **Field visits**. On one day of the workshop, the participants visited organizations such as a bank, processor, cooperative or research station. They were given a task to gather particular pieces of information for each visit, sometimes preparing a list of questions to ask beforehand. They conducted interviews, interacted with the institution's staff, made observations and gathered information. Back at the workshop venue at the end of the day, they made short presentations to the other participants on what they had learned.

- **New assignment**. The support team presented the assignment to the participants for the following months. This assignment included several forms to fill in and instructions on how to do this. For example, the assignment on business planning (given in Step 5) included a series of forms for each section in the business plan, along with detailed guidelines on how to gather and summarize information. The participants also received an example of a completed plan.

  The new assignment was always introduced through a presentation of the assignment itself, a discussion on how the participants should go about doing it, followed by a question-and-answer session. Plenty of time was allocated for participants to discuss and ask questions.

In addition, the initial workshops provided an opportunity for two other types of activities:

- **Exchange among participants**. The workshops were ideal opportunities for informal interactions among the various participants. They could share their experiences during the breaks, in the evenings, or during specially scheduled sessions. For example, the people from the Burka Gudina Farmers Cooperative asked for an opportunity to share their experiences in working with an exporter of haricot beans.

- **Administration and planning**. The workshops also enabled the support team to meet with participating organizations to plan coaching activities, deal with administrative and financial matters, and provide space to discuss any issues that had arisen.

Photo 1. Awassa workshop, June 2008: on average 70 people participated in the workshops

Assignment

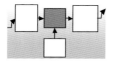

After the workshop, the participants started working on their assignments. They had three to six months to complete the assignment before the next workshop. Key elements in the assignment were:

- **Theme**. It dealt with a highly relevant theme, directly related to the ongoing work of the farmers' organization and support NGO.

- **Collaboration**. The farmers' organization and its support NGO worked together to gather and analyse the required information and write a short report on their main findings.

- **Data collection**. Each farmers' organization decided on the best way to collect the data relevant for their situation. There was no prescription from the support team on how to do this.

- **Part of regular work**. As far as possible, the data collection was incorporated in the regular activities of the farmers' organization and the support NGO.

- **Visits**. The information gathering often involved direct interaction with other chain actors and required a visit to a processing company, buyer, bank, research station, cooperative office or extension agency to interview key staff on site.

- **Reporting**. The representatives of the farmers' organization and the support NGO brought their findings to the exchange workshop. They presented the findings in a plenary or group session and discussed them with the other participants.

Photo 2. Debre Zeit workshop, June 2009: group preparing a presentation on the findings of the field assignment

Coaching

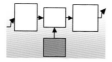

Roughly halfway between the initial and exchange workshops, the farmers' organization and their NGO were visited at least once by two members of the support team for a coaching visit. They visited the farmers' organization's office as well as some individual farmers. The coaching involved the following elements:

- **Review of status**. The coaches reviewed the status of the assignment and helped the farmers' organization and NGO to complete it.

- **Progress**. They reviewed the overall progress made in the earlier steps of the Learning Alliance, including whether the organizations had done what they stated in their action plans (see next section).

- **Collaboration**. They looked at the collaboration between the farmers' organization and the support NGO, and where needed helped improve the relationship.

- **Members' involvement**. They assessed the involvement of the members of the farmers' organization and where possible helped increase members' participation in the process. They reviewed the involvement of the members in the earlier phases of the Learning Alliance and the impact it had had on their farms, income and marketing. They also checked how far the members were involved in conducting the assignment.

- **Internal sharing**. They checked if any experiences from the Learning Alliance had been shared within the NGO. Where possible the coaches provided suggestions to enhance the dissemination of such experiences within the NGO, between different levels (between headquarters and field offices, among field offices, and with partners such as like-minded NGOs).

- **Support team**. The same members of the support team coached the farmers' organization and support NGO. This was to maintain continuity and build trust.

- **Outside support**. An outside coach was hired to help with financial services (Step 4) and business planning (Step 6). The support team lacked the specific expertise and time for coaching. All farmer organizations were visited by the same coach. This coach prepared summary reports to share his finding and recommendations with the support team.

Exchange workshop

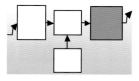

This workshop reviewed and discussed the results of the assignment. The workshop lasted for 2–3 days. The participants reflected on their experiences and on those of their peers, and on the implications for their own organizations.

- **Review of assignment**. The participants were divided into groups, and each presented the results of the assignment. The farmer organization and NGO jointly presented what they had done, and displayed the results on notice boards around the room. They also answered questions and responded to comments from the other participants. This sometimes led to animated discussions about the merits and difficulties of a particular approach or issue.

- **Summary of achievements**. One of the participants from each group summarized the activities they had done since the last workshop.

- **Impressions from the support team**. The coaches shared the insights they gained from their field visits. Based on an analysis done prior to the workshop, KIT provided comments on the results coming out of the assignments. Both presentations highlighted encouraging developments and areas for improvement.

- **Action planning**. The support team then asked the participants to plan in concrete terms what they would do next in order to put what they had learned into action. Each farmers' organization discussed with their NGO what to do, when to do it, who was responsible, what resources were needed to make it happen, and the sources of these resources. Each noted their decisions on a form with a row for each proposed activity and columns for these items. As required, the support team helped each farmers' organization to make these decisions.

- **Evaluation of progress**. The participants where asked to give their opinion on what they liked and disliked about exchange workshop but also about the Learning Alliance process so far. They provided direct feedback and suggestions to the support team. The evaluation results were presented and discussed in a plenary session at the end of the workshop.

Photo 3. Debre Zeit workshop, February 2009: practical exercises helped to discuss the roles and the power positions of different actors in the value chain

Taking the next step

Finalizing one step in the Learning Alliance ladder with an exchange workshop meant it was time to move on to the next step. For example, mapping the chain was directly followed by strengthening the chain actors, which was followed by financial and business services (see Figure 4).

In order to save time and resources, the exchange workshop for one step was followed immediately with the initial workshop of the next step: at the end of the exchange workshop, the facilitators introduced the next step. Combining an "old" with a "new" topic in one event created a dynamic turning point in the Learning Alliance process.

Wheat and maize

Bulking maize: Lalisa Walgayi Karro Gayib Cooperative

Location: Sayo, Dembi Dollo woreda, Kellem Wollega zone, Oromia state
Founded: 2005
Members: 410 (73 women)
Product: Maize
Supported by: Nekemte Catholic Secretariat, and Cordaid
Business contest: Learning strategy prize ✳

A farmers' cooperative that aims to improve its members' access to food grains during periods of shortage. It buys and stores food grains, especially maize, and sells to members, wholesalers and consumers.

Unlike much of Ethiopia, Dembi Dollo district gets enough rain to allow farmers there to grow crops. But the farmers still struggled to grow enough to feed their families all year round. Short of cash, they would sell their crops at low prices directly after the harvest. Faced with empty stores later in the year and waiting for the next harvest to come, they had to buy grain at high prices to feed their families.

The Lalisa Walgayi Karro Gayib cooperative, composed of three farmers' associations, aimed to break this vicious circle by establishing a grain bank. It filled its store by buying grain and other crops at harvest time, and selling them back to its members at reasonable prices during times of food shortage. This worked well from a food-security perspective, but the cooperative also wanted a commercial orientation to improve its own cash income and that of its members.

As a result of the Learning Alliance, the cooperative members and management decided to focus on just one crop, maize. It developed a plan for members to grow larger volumes and produce better quality. That had two benefits: it guaranteed food security for members, and it enabled the cooperative to charge traders higher prices for bulked, high-quality grain. In 2008, for the first time the cooperative met its target of ensuring food security for its members, and in 2009 it generated a surplus that gave it financial independence. It is now planning to supply regional markets and is even considering exporting grain to Kenya and Sudan.

Market mapping as a key to growth:
Alabedas Farmers' Marketing Organization

Location:	Chelanko, Jelduu woreda, West Shoa zone, Oromia state
Founded:	2001
Members:	628 (187 women)
Product:	Wheat
Supported by:	HUNDEE Oromo Grassroots Development Initiative and ICCO
Business contest:	Pro-poor strategy prize ✦

A farmers' cooperative that buys and sells wheat and provides warehousing services.

Despite a good climate and soil and an adequate capital base, the Alabedas Farmers' Marketing Organization was not making a profit. *"We almost had no market information; as a result we were not profitable,"* says Fekadu Bayisa, an executive member of the group.

After joining the Learning Alliance in 2007, the cooperative started to rethink how to be more profit-oriented. The training on value chain mapping proved crucial in encouraging the Alabedas cooperative to do some market research. *"After the training, we asked individual farmers where they sell their products and for how much. And then we followed the chain and made similar assessments along the way"*, says Fekadu. Through the research, the cooperative came into contact with two big companies: a wholesaler and a food processor. The Alabedas cooperative decided to focus on supplying wheat to these buyers.

Today the two big companies are the cooperative's loyal customers. They demand volume and quality, stimulating the cooperative to enter partnerships with research institutions to identify the best varieties to grow. Members now produce two main kinds of wheat – for pasta and for flour. They can get market information, updated every day, from the cooperative's office in Jeldu.

Chain partnership invigorates the Meja Gero Farmers' Organization

Location: Meja, Arsi Negele woreda, East Arsi zone, Oromia state
Founded: 2007
Members: 55 (15 women)
Product: Wheat
Supported by: African Development Aid Association (ADAA), and ICCO

A farmers' organization engaged in wheat buying and selling, as well as supplying fertilizers and improved seed to its members.

Traders and flour mills in Arsi know that the Meja Gero farmers supply high-quality wheat. The farmers know this too, but the quality does not bring them any reward: their grains get the same price as lower-quality, adulterated grain. The Meja Gero Farmers' Organization was established in 2006 but it had no clear idea of how to access markets, and had limited skills in business planning and financial management.

Through the Learning Alliance, Meja Gero started to create partnerships with other actors in the value chain. It joined the Uta-Wayyu Union, the largest cooperative union in the region. It borrowed ETB 50,000 and used it to buy 16 tonnes of wheat from its members. Selling the wheat allowed Meja Gero to make a profit for the first time.

After this first success, staff of ADAA and the Learning Alliance coach from SNV facilitated a meeting between Meja Gero, its business partners and local government officials to discuss market issues. This started with finger-pointing: Meja Gero farmers described their fruitless efforts to get a better price for their quality product. The flour mills had no system to measure the quality of the wheat they buy, they said, and traders competed on price with highly adulterated wheat. The mills, in turn, suspected traders and tried to negotiate a deal directly with farmers' groups. But the flour mills said that the farmers' opportunism and price manipulation by traders led to farmers side-selling their crop rather than honouring their deals with the flour mills.

The finger-pointing stopped when a representative of a malt factory in Assela explained how it had resolved a similar situation by training farmers and providing them with improved barley seeds. The factory has its own quality standards and the pricing system rewards quality. Meja Gero and ADAA were asked to continue organizing such meetings to establish transparent relationships among the chain partners. The perspective is that the flour factories should set quality standards and invest in controls. That would allow Mejo Gero to sell bulked grain of the required grades and obtain a better price. Recently, Mejo Gero has managed to sign an agreement with one of the major buyers, a flour factory in Awassa.

Meanwhile, buying fertilizers and improved seed helped Meja Gero members boost their yields from 2.8 to 3.2 tonnes per hectare. The organization has entered a formal partnership with the Melkasa Agricultural Research Centre to get technical support on seed production.

A growing source of pride: Dedie Farmers' Cooperative

Location:	Durame woreda, Kembata Tembaro zone, SNNPR state
Founded:	2001
Members:	253 members (84 women)
Product:	Wheat
Supported by:	IIRR and ICCO

A cooperative that trades its members' wheat and operates flour mills.

Adanech Arshiso's children were not impressed when she joined the Dedie farmers' cooperative. One of her daughters objected strongly to the idea: she felt that her mother's membership of "a farmers' club" was a disgrace to the family.

Adanech and four of her friends had started the cooperative so they could earn more money by selling the wheat they grew. They hoped that by pooling their output, they could have enough to sell at a higher price to wholesalers. They also wanted to provide credit to the co-op members.

Although the area is good for growing wheat, yields were low because of a lack of good seed and fertilizer. The farmers simply did not have the money to buy such inputs. The cooperative sold the wheat to local buyers, and had no information about more profitable markets. Profits were small and declining. Without proper planning or a clear financial management system, the members started to question the benefits of the cooperative.

The turning point came after the Dedie cooperative joined the Learning Alliance. The cooperative found it could sell grain at a higher price to buyers from outside. When drought hit the area, it decided to sell grain back to its members at a reasonable price. That along with a small dividend the organization was able to pay its members made other farmers realize the benefits of joining. Some 32 farmers signed up as members, bringing the total to 37. Others were still reluctant to join, as the co-op members had no solution to the biggest problem they faced: the long journey to the nearest mill to grind their grain.

A Learning Alliance-sponsored visit to a cooperative in the town of Mojo was another turning point. The Dedie cooperative decided to copy their model and install three electric mills in their area. That generated income for the cooperative and attracted more farmers – especially women – to join so they could mill their grain cheaply and avoid a long round trip to distant mills.

In the meantime, some of the cooperative leaders were replaced with people who had received training through the Learning Alliance. More professional management, better market information, a clear financial system and access to better seed followed. Armed with an incentive and the means to produce more, the farmers trebled their yields to 39 bags per hectare (3,900 kg).

Now, Adanech's daughter has asked for her forgiveness for her previous doubts. And her son is looking forward to joining the cooperative staff when he leaves school.

3 Steps in the Learning Alliance cycle

Step 1 Inception

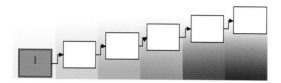

Purpose

- To present the idea of a Learning Alliance to the participating farmers' organizations and NGOs and get their support.

- To shape the initial agenda based on the participants' needs.

- To obtain formal commitment of participating organizations.

What happened

Initial workshop. The Learning Alliance started with a 3-day workshop with interested NGOs and farmers' organizations. The event was prepared by a group of people from each of the participating development partners: Agriterra, Agri-ProFocus, Cordaid, FFARM, ICCO, IIRR, KIT and SNV. It took place in Debre Zeit on 27, 28 and 30 March 2007.

The workshop included a combination of short plenary presentations followed by discussions, and group work followed by presentations. During the first two days, 35 people participated, including representatives of 14 NGOs that committed themselves to become part of the Learning Alliance. The third day concentrated on the farmers and their organizations: 26 people participated, including representatives of 18 farmers' organizations committed to take part in the Learning Alliance.

The support team introduced the Learning Alliance approach, putting it into the broader perspective of chain empowerment (see Chapter 1). The discussions that followed lead to a refinement of the approach, tailored to the Ethiopian situation. Next, an assessment was made of the participants' needs. The needs were categorized into issues related to production, to the market and structure and management of farmer organizations. A quick inventory was made how these needs related to the ongoing activities of the organizations present. The participants also described the areas where future support was deemed necessary.

It was agreed the Learning Alliance should help empower farmers' organizations in the value chain by strengthening their capacities and those of their members. The main topics to cover were identified:

- How to map the value chain and how to conduct market analysis.

- How to improve the management of a farmers' organization.

- How to deal with financial services.

- How to develop business ventures and make business plans.

- How to engage with the enabling environment.

A preliminary agenda for Learning Alliance activities was drawn up. This agenda was refined during the course of the Alliance. It was concluded that a thorough analysis of the value chain was required to get started with the Learning Alliance process. This formed the next step in climbing the Learning Alliance ladder.

What was achieved

Programme formulation. The participants, partner organizations and the support team got to know each other, were introduced to the idea of a Learning Alliance, and learned how it could be useful and how to adapt it to their own situation. They were enthusiastic and committed to the process and to working together. They jointly formulated the programme in terms of the topics to be covered, and reached agreement about their roles, responsibilities and funding arrangements.

Support for the Alliance process. This was a crucial step to generate support for the idea of a Learning Alliance and shape its agenda around the critical needs of its participating institutions and people. The workshop required intensive preparation from the organizers to properly present themselves and the idea in order to generate a genuine buy-in into the process.

Formal commitment. Representatives of NGOs and farmers' organizations signed a formal statement declaring their commitment to the Learning Alliance initiative. The development partners developed a memorandum of understanding stating their commitment to the Learning Alliance.

Examples of learning

Farmers' organizations and NGOs talked about the problems they encountered in assisting farmers to market their produce. Many participants faced similar challenges, creating solid ground for a joint learning agenda. Participants were eager to hear how a value chain perspective could be helpful in tackling their production and marketing problems.

Two issues stood out: the role and performance of traders buying the products from the farmers, and the relationship of the farmers with the NGO providing support to them and their organization.

Role of traders. The NGOs and the farmers' organizations stressed that *"farmers are very much exploited by traders, and anything that minimizes the degree of exploitation is very welcome."* They were challenged by a value chain perspective that acknowledges the role traders play (KIT and IIRR, 2008). Practical cases were presented where *"farmers could see traders as partners: if things are coordinated they can work with traders. Informed farmers can work with traders."* This generated a lively debate. The participants agreed that the Learning Alliance should pay ample attention to developing farmers' negotiation skills.

Relationship between farmers and support NGOs. The commitment of NGOs towards improving the position of farmers was acknowledged, and the practical achievements were praised. Yet some participants stressed the sustainability of the farmers and their organizations: *"Farmers have become too dependent on their NGO: it is so important that they can negotiate on their own."* This triggered a reflection among the participants to what extent the NGOs were in the "driving seat". Was the support they provided always relevant for the farmers' organizations? Or was the support the NGO provided so crucial for the farmers' organization that they were becoming too dependent? Could the farmers' organizations survive on their own without the services provided by their NGO?

Step 2 Mapping the chain

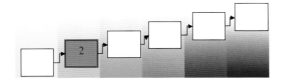

Purpose

- To get to know the value chain.

- To get to know the position of the farmer in the chain.

- To explore how to improve the position of the farmer in the chain.

What happened

Coaching. There was no initial workshop to launch Step 2. Instead, the coaches paid a visit to all farmers' organizations to introduce the assignment for mapping the chain and help them get started. The NGO supporting the farmers' organization also participated in the coaching session. The coach helped the farmers' organization and the NGO to learn together by working together. The assignment helped to make this practical.

Assignment. For their value chain mapping, each farmers' organization selected one product: the main crop in their area or a product with high market potential. The assignment reviewed in detail the characteristics of this value chain. The main elements included in the assignment were:

• Selecting a product to work on, based on experience, climate, agronomic and market conditions.

• Conducting a rapid market survey through interviewing middlemen, focusing on sales, prices, sourcing, storage, quality, supply conditions, business conditions, and chain cooperation.

• Mapping the chain: visualizing the flow of the product from farmer to consumer.

• Determining the opportunities and challenges in the chain.

• Drawing lessons from the information gathered on the farmers' position in the value chain and drafting action plans to help empowering farmers in the chain.

The coaches remained in telephone contact with most of the farmers' organizations, and provided guidance where needed. The completed assignments were sent to the coaches by regular mail. Only a few with internet access could e-mail the assignment to the coaches. A few participants brought their assignment to the exchange workshop. The Learning Alliance support team reviewed the assignments and discussed the results while preparing the exchange workshop. During that workshop the team provided feedback to the participants.

Exchange workshop. The exchange workshop was held in Addis Ababa on 7–8 November 2007. The results of the assignments were shared and discussed in small working groups. In each group, four farmers' organizations and their NGOs shared the information they collected and commented upon each other's experiences. This generated a peer-to-peer exchange of insights, revealing similarities and differences.

For the grain value chains, most of the farmers found the end market was not the problem. There was sufficient consumer demand, and prices were considered to be quite good. The main challenges farmers felt was with middlemen cheating on quality and traders working together to suppress prices at the farm gate. The larger buyers were intensely looking for high-quality supplies, and stated they would prefer direct sourcing from farmers. The farmers could improve their business by bulking their supplies, improving quality, using high-quality seeds, having access to credit and market information, and developing chain partnerships. This generated a stream of ideas for follow-up for the farmers' organizations and their supporting NGOs.

Each group summarized their discussions in plenary. The support team then provided feedback on the assignments, stressing the need to update the information continuously and to keep a close eye to its quality. The team challenged the participants by returning to the example of the cheating traders: did the farmers never themselves cheat? It is easy to blame traders as the villains in the system, but sometimes they are trapped as well in a situation dominated by mistrust: the sellers cheat; the buyers cheat; everybody expects everybody else to cheat. A value chain perspective can provide angles to tackle such situations by identifying common interests, bring the players together and search ways to lower the transaction costs for all parties. Finally, the link to practical follow-up actions was made: what would the participants do with the gained insights, what would happen with the opportunities that were detected?

The exchange workshop ended with some reflections on value chain development: what strategies were there to improve the farmers' position in the value chain? The participants discussed how the assignment could help improve the position of farmers in the value chain. The farmers' organizations then started to work with the NGOs on action plans to do this.

What was achieved

Understanding of market orientation. Farmers and NGOs became acquainted with market-oriented thinking and a private-sector perspective. They started looking at farming as part of an interlinked commercial system bringing food from "farm to fork". The assignment stimulated the participants to research the value chains they operate in, and to connect to others (such as traders and processors) doing business in the chain. Armed with a set of key questions, they gained insights into the commercial relationships as well as opportunities and problems in their chain.

Confirmation of experiences. The exchange of experiences made participants realize that others were facing similar situations and that they could learn from one another.

Action plans. Action plans were developed on how to improve farmers' position in the value chain. That exercise helped the participants to link the results of their value chain mapping to a set of concrete activities.

Examples of learning

Realization of interdependence in the value chain. One farmer remarked: *"I never realized that after I sell to the trader, my crop goes to more stages and through more hands before it finally reaches the family that eats it, and that I and all these people are in a way dependent on each other."*

Business perspective. One farmers' organization stressed that finding out for yourself who your buyers are and pro-actively ask them how they look at the business is a very good way of looking at your own organization, and even your own farm. Learning by doing triggers a shift of perspective towards looking at farming as a business.

Mapping value chains. From a somewhat abstract concept at the start, the value chain became a lively and practical idea when the participants drew maps of the value chains they operated in. This created better understanding of the position farmers take in a wider commercial system and spurred a range of ideas how to improve the linkages in the chain.

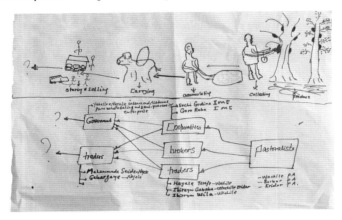

Photo 4. A value chain map drawn by farmers during the Addis Ababa exchange workshop

Step 3 Strengthening chain actors

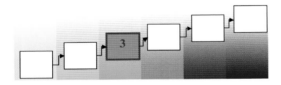

Purpose

- To reflect on the skills required to shift from a production- to a market-orientation.

- To analyse the position of farmers in the value chain and generate strategies for empowerment.

- To reflect on who will provide the services to make the change.

What happened

Initial workshop. The initial workshop for Step 3 directly followed the close of the exchange workshop of Step 2. It was held in Addis Ababa on 9 November 2007.

To introduce the next step, experiences in Ethiopia with value chain work were presented by invited speakers from the Grain Traders Association of Ethiopia, the International Food Policy Research Institute, the Ethiopian Commodity Exchange, the International

Livestock Research Institute and Apinec (an Ethiopian agro-processing company). They explained their approach in strengthening farmers' position in the value chain.

In plenary, the support team introduced the type of skills farmers and their organizations typically need to become an "empowered chain actor". Groups of farmers' organizations and NGOs then conducted self-analyses on the skills already available and those still lacking in their organizations. The groups also reflected on what kind of services were needed to provide the missing skills. They then shared their findings in plenary.

This was followed by a short plenary discussion on specific skills the participants needed to strengthen the position of farmers' in the value chain.

Assignment. The assignment was introduced in the workshop. It asked the participants to prepare:

- A business profile of the farmers' organization including crop area, product volume, percentage of output sold through the farmers' organization, and a list of buyers.

- A calculation of production costs covering inputs, labour, transport, storage, equipment and taxes.

- A calculation of selling costs including procurement, transport, marketing, labour, finance, depreciation, maintenance and taxes.

- A calculation of profit margins.

- A description of ways to improve quality involving inputs, production processes, harvesting, post-harvest handling, marketing and management.

- A description of ways to increase volume including production processes, procurement, logistics, finance, and cooperation in the chain.

- A review of the existing skills of the farmers' organization to improve quality and increase volume through changes in input procurement, production, handling, marketing, finance, management and administration.

- An analysis of the available support services instrumental in making the change in the areas of inputs supply, production processes, handling, marketing, finance, management and administration.

Coaching. Coaching visits were made to all participating farmers' organizations and NGOs to help them accomplish the assignment. In most cases, two visits were made. Due to the long distances, this was a considerable investment of time and resources. The coaches also reviewed the progress made so far in putting action plans into practice. By visiting the participants in their own area, the coaches acquired a good feeling of the conditions they were operating in, including the business and marketing challenges they faced. This knowledge was discussed with the support team and provided input into the organization of the exchange workshop.

Exchange workshop. The exchange workshop was held in Awassa on 17–19 June 2008. It started with the participants sharing and discussing the outcomes of their assignments in small working groups. This generated discussions on similarities and differences in the conditions the farmers' organizations faced, and on ways to use the collected information to improve their performance.

In plenary, the coaches reported on the visits they had made and reviewed the results of the assignment. They gave their impression of the overall progress of the Learning Alliance initiative. They particularly stressed the increased level of commitment of the farmers' organizations in the process.

The workshop included a field visit to four Sidama primary coffee cooperatives. The participants were split in four groups, each visiting two cooperatives. The groups were asked to review six specific areas of the cooperative business: internal management and administration, partnership with others, primary production process, post-harvest operations, credit and investments, and marketing and sales. Questions focused on the kind of problems encountered in each of these areas and how the problems were tackled. The cooperative managers and members were also asked what made the cooperative a successful actor in a value chain. Before visiting the cooperatives, participants were given some time to prepare their interviews.

Directly after the field visit, small groups of participants discussed the results. They presented short statements to a group of invited guests working in cooperative development. The guests were from ACDI/VOCA Ethiopia (a US-based non-profit organization promoting cooperative development in Ethiopia), the Cooperative Agency of the SNNP Region (a governmental agency supporting cooperatives), and Learning Alliance partner FFARM (a not-for-profit enterprise supporting Ethiopian farmers accessing markets). A panel discussed followed, focusing on the skills cooperatives need in the six aforementioned areas.

During the last part of the workshop, the participants reflected on what they had learned from the assignment, the coaching sessions and the exchange workshop. They identified two challenges in skill development to work on in the coming half year, determined the activities to undertake, the resources they needed, the actors to involve and kind of support required, and the timeframe.

What was achieved

Capacity improvements. Farmers' organizations and NGOs recognized the key capacities needed to improve the position of farmers in the value chain. They reflected on what is required to improve their skills. The field visit gave the participants an opportunity to learn from some of the most successful farmer cooperatives in the country.

Further exchange. The participants got to know each other better, which facilitated exchange and dialogue. The support team gained more experience in working together, which facilitated the organization of the workshops. They experimented with putting new elements into the workshop, such as an excursion, a panel discussion.

Learning from practice. Participants got a better feeling of the subject matter and could relate it better to their day-to-day reality, making the Learning Alliance more relevant for them. The field excursion made the subject material livelier, and direct interactions with cooperative members, managers and administrators outside the classroom contributed to the success of the exchange workshop.

Examples of learning

Advantages and disadvantages of cooperatives. Coffee cooperatives and their unions are considered to be among the most successful cases of the cooperative movement in Ethiopia. By talking to the managers, members and administrators, the participants gained direct insights in the functioning of these organizations. One of their strong features is the size of the business and the ability of the organizations to raise a large amount of working capital, from their own as well as from external sources. An element to be improved was the service delivery of the unions: the cooperatives complained that unions' operational costs were too high, putting pressure on the price they received. Some cooperative members felt they were forced to sell to the union, whereas alternatives might offer them better prices.

Photo 5: Awassa workshop, June 2008: field visits were an important element of the workshops, escaping the classroom, and connecting to farmer and business reality

Step 4 Finance and business services

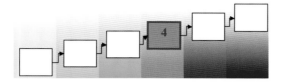

Purpose

- To review how to secure finance to increase working and investment capital for farmers' organizations.

- To assess which business services are required to improve business performance of farmers' organizations.

What happened

Initial workshop. The initial workshop was held on 20 June 2008 in Awassa. It dealt with the role of financial and business services to boost the performance of farmers' organizations, thereby strengthening their position in the value chain.

The support team gave a presentation on practical experiences with financial and business services. Financial services include short-term and longer-term loans generally provided by a bank or a microfinance institution. Business services deal with improving business performance. This might involve upgrading business operations (such as procurement, sales, quality control), as well as improving the skills of farmers, administrators, managers, etc.

Assignment. The farmers' organizations analysed, with the help of their NGOs, their internal financial systems and their past and current financial results. It asked the participants to prepare for a visit to a financial institution (a bank or a microfinance organization) to request a loan. What kind of information would a bank employee need to get from a farmers' organization in order to start a loan application process? Is that information readily available in the farmers' organization? If not, what needs to be done to obtain that information?

Coaching. In this step, the coaching was not done by the regular team of coaches because of time constraints and the recognition that financial services are best handled by a specialist. The farmers' organizations and NGOs helped to choose this specialist. Mr. Getnet Haile was requested to do the coaching, a man with ample experience in rural finance in Ethiopia.

Apart from helping the farmers to fulfill the assignment, the financial coach reviewed the internal financial procedures operated by each farmers' organization. He gave feedback to improve these financial systems, focusing on improving transparency and accountability whilst stressing processes that are simple, cheap and easy to implement. With a properly functioning internal financial system, it is easier for the organization to attract external funding. The coach discussed how to do this with the farmers and their NGO. The coach wrote a short supervision report for each farmers' organization providing tailor-made recommendations on how to improve their financial procedures. On the basis of this, each organization prepared an action plan to improve its financial system, covering aspects such as stock keeping, bookkeeping and invoices.

Exchange workshop. The exchange workshop was held in Debre Zeit on 24–26 February 2009. It started with a short recap of the Learning Alliance process: what had been achieved so far, the stage the Learning Alliance had now reached, and what still had to be done. This was followed by a role-playing game where participants took on the role of a particular actor in a value chain. Small groups of participants then shared lessons from the assignments and the coaching visit. The support team and the financial coach provided feedback to the groups.

In a short plenary session, the financial coach shared his main insights from his coaching visits. The support team also summarized their observations from the assignments and pointed out the need to translate the insights gained from the assignments and coaching visits into concrete action plans.

Small groups of participants visited a bank and a microfinance institution in the town of Debre Zeit to find out how a farmers' organization could get a loan from them and how different their response was compared to financial institution interviewed for the assignment. Each group prepared questions beforehand to guide their interviews with the bank managers, financial officers and administrators they met. After the visit, each group prepared a short summary of what they had learned. This was followed by a panel discussion with a representative of each of the institutions visited.

A presentation by the Dutch rural finance organization, Terrafina, introduced a study of the provision of financial services in Ethiopia. Further sessions covered practical experiences on value chain finance in the agricultural sector (by KIT) and an introduction to business services (by KIT and FFARM). Business services help chain actors to improve their businesses in such areas as marketing, technology, product design, logistics, management, accounting, and human resource management. Service providers may be commercial companies, NGOs or public agencies.

To illustrate the business services available in Ethiopia for the agricultural sector, a "market place" was organized where six key Ethiopian service providers presented their expertise and services, the clients they had worked with, and the conditions for hiring them. Small groups of participants visited service providers of their choice in "speed dating" sessions. The service providers were seated in different corners of the room; the participants asked them questions, heard about the services they offered, learned about the conditions and fees, and listened to examples of the support provided. After 20 minutes, the participants rotated to meet another service provider. There were three rounds of visits, enabling all participants to visit three service providers. A plenary discussion followed on the lessons from this speed dating.

The workshop ended with an evaluation: the participants gave their opinions on the workshop and the Learning Alliance process so far. The support team responded to the issues raised and where needed adjusted the organisation of the next step.

What was achieved

Financial management. The farmers' organizations improved their financial administration, both in terms of internal transparency and to prepare for accessing external finance. They learned what is required to get a loan from a financial institution. The financial coach visited all the farmers' organizations, reviewed each one, and suggested ways to improve their financial systems.

Business services. The farmers obtained a clear idea of what business services are, what they can do, what they cost, and what results they can bring. The "market place" format where the service providers ("suppliers") explained their services to small groups of potential clients ("customers"), worked very well. Participants appreciated this informal opportunity to talk to the providers.

Examples of learning

Supply and demand for services. One business service provider introduced the kind of support he offered to farmers and their organizations. One farmer liked what he heard, but was not pleased when he learned about the cost: *"I like your services but I can't afford them: why are you so expensive?"*, he said. The service provider and the farmer were connecting to each others' realities, explaining to the other how their business operates.

Photo 6. DebreZeit workshop, February 2009: providers of business services explained how they can help farmers to become better businessmen

Step 5 Business planning

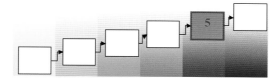

Purpose

- To help farmers' organizations to make a business plan.

- To analyse in a systematic way how a farmers' organization functions as a commercial entity.

What happened

Initial workshop. The initial workshop took place on 27 February 2009 in Debre Zeit. It introduced the idea of business planning and how to make a business plan. The link was made with the business plan contest: the final step (Step 6) in the Learning Alliance. The prospect of entering in a contest with a cash prize created excitement among the participants.

Assignment. The main task in the assignment centred on discussions and negotiations with buyers. For this assignment, the farmers' organizations were divided into three categories, reflecting their current business situation and position in the chain. Each category was given a slightly different assignment to suit their situation:

- **Integrating farmers' organizations**. These organizations had developed active commercial linkages with buyers (traders, processors, supermarkets etc.). Their assignment was to develop a joint "chain partnership plan" with these actors, describing how they together could improve their business.

- **Emerging farmers' organizations**. These organizations had invested strongly in exploring chain relations, but so far had not developed durable commercial linkages with other chain actors. Their assignment was to gather ideas from their buyers, suppliers and service providers on how to improve the organization's performance as a business partner.

- **Kick-starting farmers' organizations**. These organizations were just starting to explore linkages with chain actors. They did not yet see themselves as a commercial enterprise, or were in remote locations where it was difficult to identify alternative markets. Their assignment was to develop an "enterprise development plan" describing how they would improve their situation.

Coaching. The coaches visited most of the farmers' organizations in the field; the others were contacted by telephone. With the farmers and their NGO, the coaches reviewed the status and results of the assignment and provided support to help them complete the assignment. In some cases the coaches participated in and facilitated the conversations between the organization and their buyer.

Exchange workshop. The exchange workshop took place in Ambo on 1–3 September 2009. After a short recap of the Learning Alliance process so far, small groups of participants discuss the results of their assignments. This was followed by a plenary session discussing commonalities.

A field visit was organized to three private companies (a small oil-processing plant, a large flour mill and a mid-sized bakery) and one cooperative union (Ambo Cooperative Union). The main goal of this visit was to review how these enterprises plan their businesses and how that could help the farmers' organizations to make their own business plans. Before the visit, the participants prepared questions to ask during the interviews. Afterwards, small groups exchanged experiences and reflected on what they learned. It appeared that not all the enterprises visited had a clear business objective, and that these were performing quite badly.

Two farmers' organizations presented their experiences with strengthening market linkages. The Gole Roge Farmers Marketing Organization introduced its partnership with a consumer association in marketing teff. The Burka Gudina Cooperative explained how it sold haricot beans under contract to ACOS Ethiopia, a subsidiary of an Italian company specialized in the production and sale of vegetables and pulses. In both cases the linkages were facilitated by the support NGO, the Centre for Development Initiatives. These presentations generated a lot of feedback from the other participants, triggering a lively debate.

Sessions followed on the importance of an enabling environment for doing business, and the role of gender relations in value chains. Interest in these two topics had been expressed earlier on in the Learning Alliance process. For each topic there was a short plenary presentation, followed by a game, group work or a discussion.

The session on the enabling environment identified the main factors promoting and hampering private sector development in Ethiopia. The different national, regional and local governmental agencies involved in this field were identified. The contributions of the private sector and civil society in improving the business environment were also discussed.

The session on gender stressed the different positions that men and women have in agricultural value chains. To reach women as much as men, it is important to understand these differences. Key issues include land rights for women, decision making in the household (who decides on what), relations between different actors in the chain (what positions are typically taken by men, which by women), and women's positions in the management and decision making of farmers' organizations. The session ended with a discussion on the roles, tasks and positions that are typically "female" and "male" in rural Ethiopia.

The exchange workshop ended with an evaluation of the event and an assessment by the participants of the Learning Alliance process so far.

Business planning. The farmers' organizations got a clear idea of business planning and how to use a business plan in improving their commercial performance. The interactions with entrepreneurs strengthened their perspective on approaching farming as a business.

Tailored assignments. Tailoring the assignments to three categories of farmers' organizations ensured that each organization would be able to undertake activities that would be most useful.

Pro-active engagement. Two farmers' organizations asked to present their experiences during the exchange workshop. This showed that the participants, and particularly the farmers, had become much more pro-active during the course of the Learning Alliance. Peer to peer exchange had gained in momentum.

Examples of learning

Integrating farmers' organizations. In this group, the Burka Gudina organization had made an agreement with a bean exporter. The company committed to provide the Burka Gudina with inputs and to buy the beans it produced, while Burka Gudina committed to sell to the company.

Emerging farmer' organizations. The Dimbira farmers' organization sold all its coffee to the Coffee Cooperative Union. By improving its financial management (by reducing the delay in payment and attracting outside finance) it generated enough working capital to buy all its members' coffee. By increasing its sales, it strengthened its relation with the Cooperative Union.

Kick-starting farming organizations. Goro Roba and Sochi Gudina farmers' organizations connect to a trader in incense and gum. Before, none of the local traders wanted to talk about partnerships. But after agreeing to pursue a different approach that emphasized commercial relationships and mutual benefits, the organizations were able to make a deal with a big trader from outside the area.

Step 6 Business contest

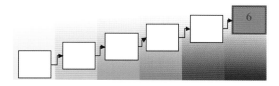

Purpose

- To improve business through writing a business plan.

- To get feedback from a professional jury on the business plan.

- To participate in a business plan contest with the chance of winning a prize to be invested in the business.

What happened

Initial workshop. The initial workshop was held in Ambo on 4 September 2009. A plenary session covered how to write a business plan for a farmers' organization. It detailed aspects such as the need for consultations with members and clear leadership, the structure of the plan (the business idea, organizational set-up, a marketing plan, an operational plan, a financial planning and risk analysis), and the risks farmers' organizations have to deal with. It gave examples of business plans and tips on how to develop them.

Assignment. The business plan contest, the final step of the Learning Alliance process, was then introduced. The organization of the contest and the criteria for selecting the winning proposals were discussed, and detailed contest guidelines were distributed in Amharic and English.

Box 2 shows the business plan format given to the participants.

The contest prizes were outlined:

- The farmers' organization with the highest score would receive the first prize (€14,000), with prizes of €12,000 and €10,000 going to the runners up.

- Five special prizes of €6,000 each would be awarded for the best learning strategy, attraction of outside funding, best pro-poor impact, most balanced gender strategy, and best approach to capacity development.

- All the farmers' organizations entering a plan in the contest would be given €500 as a reward for their effort.

The jury used 10 criteria to evaluate the business plans; each criterion was marked from 1 (poor) to 10 (excellent):

- Viable and innovative ways improving production, productivity, market access and profitability.

- Inclusion of poorer households.

- Contribution to gender equality.

- Increased household income and improved livelihoods.

- Strengthening capacities of chain actors and chain supporters.

Box 2.   Business plan format

1. Background (maximum 4 pages)
A. Current situation of the farmers' organization:
- Main characteristics of the farmer organization (age, number of members, male/female ratio, etc.)
- Product, productivity, processing (cleaning, grading, packaging, etc.)
- Unique features of the product
- Prices and profitability
- Market, traders and consumers

B. Constraints related to:
- Production and productivity
- Markets
- Collaboration in the chain
- Institutional environment

C. Strengths and weaknesses
D. Opportunities for chain development and the role of the farmers' organization

2. Strategy (maximum 3 pages)
A. Description of the activities to seize the opportunities
B. Expected results related to:
- Strengthened capacities of the farmers' organization and its members
- Farmers' organization playing a leading role in value chain development
- New collaborative arrangements among chain actors
- New collaborative arrangements between chain actors and providers of services
- New clients, access to remunerative markets and increased sales
- Access to inputs and credits
- Increased production, higher productivity, lower costs, better quality, increased value adding
- Balanced gender relations
- Inclusion of the poor

3. Budget (maximum 3 pages)
A. Activity based budget including:
- A cost-benefit analysis
- The funding strategy
- Utilization of the price money

4. Sustainability (maximum 1 page)
A. Support for capacity strengthening and other follow-up activities
B. A risk analysis and measures to mitigate risks.

- Inclusion of local entrepreneurs committed to invest time and money.

- Application of lessons learned in the Learning Alliance.

- Realistic funding arrangements including contribution of own resources.

- Accessing loans for the necessary investments.

- Utilization of the prize money.

Coaching. The farmers' organizations and their NGOs were asked to suggest a coach who could help them with their business plan. All opted to continue working with Getnet Haile, the financial coach who had visited them in Step 4. Apart from being a specialist in rural finance, he also has a strong profile in developing business plans. He visited all farmers' organizations once again. In presence of the NGO, the main arguments of the proposed business idea were reviewed, and the coach advised how to improve the proposal's business orientation, strengthen its financial implications, and stress how it would enhance collaboration in the value chain. He wrote a report summarizing each visit, which he shared with the farmers' organization, their NGO and the organizers of the Learning Alliance.

Exchange workshop. The exchange workshop took place on 15–17 February 2010 in Addis Ababa. The agenda included the presentation of the business plans to the jury, writing stories about the lessons from the Learning Alliance process, an award ceremony for the contest, and the closure of the Learning Alliance.

All 18 farmers' organizations entered a business plan in the contest. A representative of each organization presented its plan to the jury and responded to their questions, comments and suggestions. The jury consisted of six professionals with wide experience in the private sector in Ethiopia (half were themselves Ethiopian entrepreneurs). The plans were sent to the jury members one month before the workshop to give them time to read all the plans. The jury was split in two groups, and discussed the business plans in parallel sessions. After all business plans were presented, the jury ranked them and agreed on the prize winners.

Annex 3 lists the winners, the main elements of their business plans, and a projection of the extra income they hoped to gain.

While the jury was meeting each representative, the remaining participants told and wrote stories about what they had learned from the Learning Alliance initiative. A group of six Ethiopian journalists helped each farmers' organization and their NGO to write a short story. After the workshop each underwent another round of editing. The stories are printed in between the chapters in this book.

The workshop ended with the award ceremony. The hall was covered with posters summarizing the business plans. The jury gave a general impression of the contest, followed by detailed feedback on the individual business plans. *"The plans show that the Learning Alliance has been useful"*, the jury said; *"most business plans were realistic, feasible and convincing. The best business plans were simple, specific, well budgeted and clearly focused. Some very innovative business models were seen in honey, linseed, incense and gum"*. According to the jury some farmers' organizations were inclined to do more chain activities themselves, but the additional costs and risks of these chain activities required more attention and reflection. The jury found that the farmers' organizations had enhanced their business orientation and created new market linkages and arrangements for adding value. All the prize winners were invited to receive their certificates for their prize money.

The contest ended with a cocktail and dinner, the official closure of the Learning Alliance.

Business contest. The business plan contest clearly had a positive impact on raising the business acumen of the farmers' organizations and their supporting NGOs. At the start the idea of such a contest was debated among the Learning Alliance members (development partners, NGOs and farmers' organizations alike). Competition is generally not part of the NGO approach, and "keeping the group together" and not dropping the weaker farmers' organizations was considered crucial. Gradually however, the idea prevailed that organizations had to be able to compete if they were to be successful and resilient. Attitudes among the partners shifted from resistance to seeing the contest as a good idea to strengthen entrepreneurship of farmers, their organizations and the NGOs supporting them.

The human side of business plans. Through making a business plan the participants became acquainted with a systematic, business-oriented way to look at their operations and those of their organization. The coach reinforced this. The participants also realized a written business plan needs to be backed up by the right kind of people to implement it. For the jury, as with potential funders and investors, the "human" side was very important in ranking the business plans: were there enough entrepreneurial skills to implement the idea? The farmers' organizations with the most entrepreneurial people made the best impression. Jury members sensed the trustworthiness and credibility of the leadership from the oral presentation rather than from the written plan.

Award ceremony. The ceremony was a nice way of ending the Learning Alliance initiative. It gave recognition to those participants that were the most active in the Alliance and the most business-oriented at the same time.

Examples of learning

First prize ✳ Ifabari (teff). According to the jury, the Ifabari farmers' organization went through a remarkable learning cycle, leading to a high-quality business plan. Its plan stood out in terms of its simplicity and clear focus. Ifabari opted to strengthen its core business (marketing teff) while at the same time improving key chain activities such as input supply and diversifying market outlets. During the presentation of the plan, the jury was pleasantly surprised by the great passion, enthusiasm and entrepreneurial vision expressed by Ifabari's leaders. The prize money will give the organization a further boost to become even more productive, sustainable and profitable.

Second prize ✳ Gole Roge (teff). Gole Roge managed to develop contractual arrangements where its members generate a sustainable supply to a number of reliable buyers, including processors and consumer associations. The business plan clearly described how to improve product quality and which activities would add value to their product. An interesting feature of the plan was the idea to explore a joint venture with a business and a consumer association to generate money to invest in processing.

Third prize ✳ Agama (honey). Agama had established a stable relationship with a company called Apinec Agro Industry by providing high-quality honey. The jury was impressed by its realistic projections on how its business could grow further. Agama's plan was one of the few that budgeted the costs of training. Agama had clearly identified its challenges, such as a lack of financial capacity and infrastructure, and it was honest in expressing its doubts on how these should be best tackled. Likewise, it recognized it needed to further develop its value chain and strengthen its position in it, but was still searching how to do so. Its relationship with a sole buyer was a strong asset but it also realized the risk of this buyer withdrawing.

Photo 7: Addis Ababa workshop, February 2010: the award ceremony praises Ifabari for winning the business plan contest

Dairy and coffee

Finding new clients, negotiating better deals:
Biruh Tesfa Dairy Producers' Cooperative

Location:	Addis Alem, Ejera woreda, West Shoa zone, Oromia state
Founded:	2004
Members:	60 members (10 women)
Product:	Dairy
Supported by:	Self Help Africa (SHA), and ICCO

A dairy cooperative that bulks and sells its members' milk.

"My wife used to sell milk at ETB 2.50 per litre", says Lemma Worku. *"I started asking, ' Why so little?' So I gathered a petition from the nearby dairy farmers and protested openly. The big firms that bought milk from us refused to take milk from me. Once 60 litres of milk was ruined because of this. The neighbourhood dogs enjoyed the milk!"*

At the time, the large milk buyers were in a very powerful position. They bought mainly from a few favoured producers, and had no fixed place or time to collect the milk. That allowed them to set very low prices: producers who were lucky enough to meet a buyer accepted the price offer for fear of having to take their milk home. Lemma persisted, though. He and 15 other dairy producers formed the Biruh Tesfa Dairy Production Cooperative in 2004. "Biruh Tesfa" means "bright hope", but at first the members did not know how to overcome their problems. *"We just acted on common sense, without really having a clear vision of what to do and how to do it,"* says one member of the cooperative.

Through the Learning Alliance, the farmers were able to study their value chain, analyse their costs, share experiences with other farmer groups, and plan what to do. They realized that they did not have to wait for the buyers to come to them: they could seek out customers on their own. They now sell milk to hotels, restaurants and schools in the town of Addis Alem. They supply milk on credit to local civil servants, and collect the money on paydays. A litre of milk now sells for ETB 5. *"Today one of the big buyers comes to our processing place to buy milk"*, says Lemma. *"We fixed the price for them and they take it."*

The group has also started processing unsold milk to make cheese, butter and yoghurt. Not a litre is wasted. Their earlier assumption that processing milk would not be profitable has been proved wrong: they actually make more money from processed products than from fresh milk. A 22-litre churn of fresh milk fetches ETB 110; when converted into butter and cheese, it can fetch at least ETB 135. To boost sales, the co-op takes samples of its products to potential buyers. After receiving a 5 kg sample, one hotel placed an order for 30 kg of cheese and butter a day.

"Now, we are confident", says Lemma, now the co-op's chairperson. *"The Learning Alliance taught us that we can do many things. We have learned how to access the local market. We are no longer afraid that our milk goes wasted."*

Including women in the dairy business: Gelgel Area Dairy Producers' Cooperative

Location:	Holeta, Walmara woreda, West Shoa zone, Oromia state
Founded:	2004
Members:	41 members (3 women)
Product:	Dairy
Supported by:	Self Help Africa (SHA), and ICCO

A dairy cooperative that bulks and sells its members' milk.

Many households in rural Ethiopia own one or two cows. It is usually the women who look after them: cleaning the barn, bringing feed, or taking them to pasture. They do the milking and processing it into butter, cheese and yoghurt too. But when it comes to selling milk, the men take over. Many women carry the milk to the customer, but merely act as messengers: it is the men who collect the money.

Things are gradually changing thanks to the Gelgel Area Dairy Cooperative. *"We didn't allow our wives to come to the place where we sold the milk. We just thought women have no place in a business. We had forgotten that it is they who milked the cow and made butter"*, says Alemu, a cooperative member.

The cooperative was founded in 2004 by 10 dairy farmers who wanted to break their dependence on the two dairies that dominated the value chain. They started selling their milk to Faitu, a local woman who processed and sold it. Profits were meagre, but the farmers said it was better than throwing their milk away. When Faitu quit the dairy business, the two dairies refused to buy the milk from Gelgel. The farmers were left without a customer, and the cooperative stopped working.

The Learning Alliance has turned things around. Gelgel again started buying milk from its members, and sells it to local people and to hotels in the area. It began by offering farmers ETB 4 per litre, ETB 0.5 more than the price paid by the dairies. That attracted producers and gave the cooperative the volume of milk it needed to attract more customers. It also forced the dairies to match this price. Gelgel raised its price to ETB 4.50, forcing the dairies again to follow suit.

Higher prices have given farmers more profit. *"We couldn't even buy fodder with the profit we used to get. Now we get up to ETB 1 profit per litre"*, says Alemu. The cooperative now collects about 140 litres of milk a day. It sells about half fresh, and sends the rest for processing.

Although the male members now appreciate the important role that women play in the milk business, there are still only three women members in the cooperative. The men know that it is the women who care for the cattle, do the milking and keep equipment clean. Gelgel pays a trained woman ETB 300 a month to process its milk. But if Gelgel is to prosper, it needs more women members, and women to play a bigger role in the organization.

Improving coffee quality: Dimbira Coffee Farmers' Cooperative

Location: Dimbira, Chenna woreda, Kaffa zone, SNNPR state
Founded: 2000
Members: 243 members (84 women)
Product: Coffee
Supported by: Jima Bonga Catholic Secretariat, and Cordaid

A cooperative of farmers who produce specialty coffee.

Coffee originated in Ethiopia, and it is the country's most important export commodity. But until recently, the country was not known for the quality of its beans. That is beginning to change as a result of a new emphasis on producing a high-quality product. The best coffee comes from wild varieties growing in the forest, rather than "improved" cultivars in plantations. As its name implies, the Dimbra Forest Coffee Farmers' Cooperative is a group of farmers who produce the best sort, "forest coffee".

But the right varieties and growing conditions are not enough: the coffee cherries also have to be picked when they are ripe, and care is needed to avoid contamination by sticks, stones and other foreign matter. And farmers must have enough coffee bushes to earn a decent living. The Dimbra cooperative has been helping its members improve quality through a combination of awareness raising, training and strict controls. It teaches its members to pick only the red cherries, dry them on a wire mesh and put them into standard sacks. A taskforce of local people and partner institutions inspects each delivery: if someone is caught supplying cherries that have been picked green, that person's coffee is burnt in public. As a result, no one dares coming to the market with green coffee. Committees have been elected in each village to handle quality issues, and quality is a common topic at village meetings. The quality of the coffee delivered to the cooperative has improved significantly as a result of all these measures.

Berhanu Gebreyes is an example of the Dimbra's success. He used to harvest only ETB 3,000 worth of low-quality coffee from his 2,000 bushes. This meagre income meant he could hardly afford to educate his dozen children. But in June 2008, as part of a Learning Alliance workshop on "strengthening chain actors", he visited coffee farmers near Awassa. He saw that almost three-quarters of each field he visited was covered with coffee. That encouraged him and other members of Dimbra to learn how to multiply forest coffee seeds and increase their output. Over the last 3 years he has transplanted 4,000 seedlings, trebling his income from each harvest. He aims to plant 4 hectares of his 7-hectare farm to coffee. He can now afford to educate his children; four of them now go to university.

4 Results

Farmers and their organizations

The Learning Alliance helped the participating farmers and their organizations in two ways. First, it strengthened the farmers' business skills. This involved analysing markets and value chains, identifying potential buyers, appealing to them with tempting business propositions, negotiating with them on a more equal footing, and striking a deal with them. It also meant upgrading the financial administration and overall management of the farmers' organizations. Second, the farmers and their organizations were able to earn more profits through higher sales volumes and better prices.

Throughout the Learning Alliance process, the farmers were asked for their views on the relevance and impact of the Learning Alliance. Their suggestions for improvements helped the organizers assess and adjust the Learning Alliance process. During the final evaluation the farmers were asked to mention the most important change they had experienced as a result of the Learning Alliance. The five most popular responses were as follows:

Look at farming as a business. The farmers shifted from a pure production-oriented to a more market-oriented perspective. This had implications for individual farmers as well as their organizations: how to operate as commercial entity? The Learning Alliance provided tools to make this shift.

Go out and analyse your market and review your position in it. A business attitude is not enough; it is still necessary to collect and analyse information, and make decisions that will improve performance. The field assignments helped the farmers analyse their markets and value chains. Calculating the costs, benefits and margins created a clearer understanding of what makes money and what does not. Since markets change this needs to be done regularly. Farmers came up with ideas of how to improve their situation in their markets and chains, and looked for opportunities to do so.

Pro-actively develop business relations with existing and new buyers. The farmers reviewed their relation with their buyers. Some farmers' organizations actively looked for new clients to get better deals. Six of the 18 organizations started to streamline their activities to better connect to buyers' needs and preferences (particularly responding to interests expressed by traders and processors). Instead of waiting for buyers to approach them, farmers approached new potential customers, offering them persuasive commercial deals. Some organizations started negotiations with new buyers, and some struck deals.

All the 18 business plans entering the contest (see Chapter 3) included activities focusing on developing better business relations.

Get services that improve your business skills. The farmers developed a clearer view of the services they needed to become better entrepreneurs. They realized that generic support in building their basic organizational and production capacities was not sufficient. They emphasized business-specific services to tackle technical and commercial problems, such as improving production quality, streamlining financial administration in line with the requirements of credit providers, or getting help in negotiations with buyers. Of the nine prize winners in the contest, four formulated demands for specific business services in their business plans.

Increase sales and profits. Ultimately, what is needed is an increase in sales and income, both for individual farmers and the farmers' organization. The Learning Alliance support team was not able to measure changes in households. Yet, as can be seen in the 18 short stories in this book, most organizations increased their sales or laid a solid foundation to do so in the near future. In several cases, farmers switched to a new, more profitable crops or increased their cropping area. New business deals were realized that offered higher sales volumes and better prices. Some farmers' organizations reported improved financial figures in terms of increased working capital or higher sales volume and profit.

Chain empowerment strategies

Viewed through the chain empowerment framework presented in Chapter 1, the 18 farmers' organizations opted for different strategies in terms of chain activities (vertical integration) and chain management (horizontal integration). The nine organizations winning prizes in the business plan contest applied the following chain empowerment strategies (Figure 6):

❶ Upgrading as a chain actor: Lalisa Walgayi Karro Gayib (learning prize).

❷ Adding value through vertical integration: Wollela (capacity development prize), Goro Roba and Socchi Gudina (gender prize).

❸ Developing chain partnerships: Ifabari (first prize), Agama (third prize), and Alabedas (pro-poor prize).

❹ Developing ownership over the chain: Gole Roge (second prize) and Burka Gudina (funding strategy prize).

Breaking up chain development pathways into two dimensions helped the farmer organizations to think about what kind of strategies would improve their position in the value chain. The variety in strategies chosen reflects the different products and markets the farmers engage in as well as the different situations faced by their organizations.

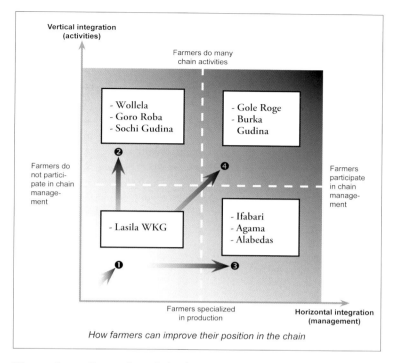

Figure 6.   Strategies of the business contest prize winners

Support NGOs

The support NGOs participating in the Learning Alliance considered the exposure to the value chain approach as the most important element of initiative. They gained knowledge and their staff developed skills in applying the concept. The NGOs detected two new roles for them in value chain development: providing business-related services to farmers' organizations, and facilitating commercial partnerships among farmers' organizations and buyers.

New knowledge. For most NGOs, linking a market and business focus to the value chain concept was a new approach. The Learning Alliance enabled them to learn about this new concept and to experiment with it through their existing working relations with farmers' organizations. It helped them make the shift from production orientation towards market-oriented support.

New skills. NGO staff gained skills in areas as chain mapping, calculation of costs, benefits and margins and making a business plan. The NGOs now use Learning Alliance approaches such as the field assignments and coaching techniques in their work with farmers' organizations. Overall, the NGO staff gained confidence in answering farmers' questions about business.

Business-oriented services for farmers. Responding to the need expressed by farmers to become more entrepreneurial, the NGOs experimented with delivering business services. These services included elements covered in the Learning Alliance such as the calculation of cost, benefit and margins, exploring new markets and identifying what is needed to supply these, upgrading the farmers' organizations' financial procedures, professionalizing cooperative management towards business principles, and joint actions to improve the farmers' position in the value chain.

Facilitating commercial partnerships. The NGOs recognized a need for facilitating contacts, communication, negotiations and finalizing deals among farmers and buyers. As the actors have different perspectives and interests, such relations do not come easily, and the NGOs realized they could play a role in facilitating them. This is a new area for most of the NGOs. Most had staff with a lot of field experience who understood the farmers' perspective, but had limited exposure to the buyers' perspective. That meant that the staff needed to strengthen their overall business acumen. Taking part in the Learning Alliance laid a foundation for this. Several of the stories in this book relate experiences of the farmers' organizations and support NGOs in making deals with new buyers; some mention deals with seed suppliers to access high-quality seeds and improved varieties.

The NGOs had long-standing working relationships with the farmers' organizations they supported: in many cases the NGO had helped farmers found the organization. The NGO staff had a very strong commitment to improve the farmers' lives. But seeing things purely from the farmers' perspective often meant they saw traders and other buyers as enemies who cheated or exploited the farmers. Through the Learning Alliance, the NGO staff came to acknowledge the farmers' longer-term need for buyers: looking beyond this season to the years to come. They learned from traders how farmers sometimes cheat. They realized that building trust would smooth the transactions between farmers and buyers, and that longer-term commercial relations would generate mutual benefits.

Evidence that NGOs had changed their attitudes towards traders appeared when six of them brought a buyer to the business planning workshop (step 5). The NGOs had helped the buyers to develop relationships with the farmers' organization, and the buyers were interested enough to accompany them at the workshop

After the close of the Learning Alliance, most NGOs decided to continue working in the field of value chains, and mentioned this in their annual and strategy plans. At least nine NGOs redefined their support roles in the area of entrepreneurship development and included specific references to value chain development and empowerment of farmers in such chains. A number of NGOs reported that they had replicated in some form the Learning Alliance process with other groups of farmers, involving other crops and other areas. A review of progress reports of six NGOs revealed that they extended their support to no less than 115 farmers' organizations.

Development organizations

The Learning Alliance impacted the development organizations in two ways: it changed individual organizations, and encouraged them to work together in a network.

FFARM used the training materials on value chain development for its consultancy assignments. In addition, it attracted donor founding to set up a Learning Alliance involving a smaller group of participants in one district.

IIRR already had a long-standing working relation with KIT, organizing writeshops and producing books on value chain development (KIT et al, 2006; KIT and IIRR, 2008; KIT and IIRR, 2010). In addition, it started to offer a course on value chain development for East Africa using a selection of elements from the Learning Alliance initiative.

For **KIT** the Learning Alliance was a logical next step of its chain empowerment approach (KIT et al., 2006). KIT was interested to experiment with applying this approach in a learning-by-doing cycle with farmers' organizations. KIT staff gained insights into Ethiopian agriculture and rural development, triggering ideas how value chain development can play a role to support this.

SNV joined the Learning Alliance as it was complementary to its economic development programme (particularly its "Business Organizations and their Access to Markets" programme). As it mainly applies a "pull" strategy where market dynamics are brought to farmers, SNV was interested to see how the Learning Alliance could make a difference by following a "push" strategy where farmers get prepared to better deal with market forces.

ICCO participated in the Learning Alliance to help achieve its goal to strengthen the market and private sector focus in its Ethiopian programme. The Learning Alliance coincided with the start of a comprehensive capacity building programme through which ICCO trained all its partner organizations in Ethiopia. Most of ICCO's partners started as cereal banks concentrating on reaching food security for their members. Now, they also embrace commercial objectives and are developing into farmers' marketing organizations.

Cordaid also took part in the Learning Alliance to further develop the market orientation of its long-term partners in Ethiopia. These partners were quite successful in adopting the value chain approach and were able to improve the performance of the farmer groups they were working with. Unfortunately, a diminishing resource base has forced Cordaid to phase out its entrepreneurship programme in Ethiopia. Nevertheless, elements of the Learning Alliance approach are used in other development and emergency programmes the organization is funding in the country.

Agriterra joined the Learning Alliance as an entry point for a new cooperative support programme in Ethiopia. The Alliance connected it to key farmers' organizations, their supporters and government agencies. Agriterra extended its existing partnership with SNV on cooperative development to include Ethiopia. It is now quickly building up its own portfolio of work in the country.

The **Agri-ProFocus** office coordinated the Learning Alliance, functioning as the central hub for the network members and the other organizations involved in the initiative. The Learning Alliance was the first joint action and learning trajectory of Agri-ProFocus in Ethiopia. During the first years, it functioned as a reference for how an Agri-ProFocus partnership could work in practice. It so influenced joint actions in other countries, such as Rwanda.

Increased Networking. Benefits have emerged from working together as a network. The Learning Alliance made it easier for staff to contact people from other organizations, particularly when working on Ethiopia. This was true for the participants based in Ethiopia but also for the organizations based in the Netherlands.

Thanks to their work together in the Alliance, SNV and ICCO set up a "competency pool", where they trained a group of Ethiopian development professionals as value chain analysts and facilitators. The idea to organize this initiative emerged between SNV and ICCO alongside the Learning Alliance trajectory.

The Learning Alliance streamlined a number of similar training activities in the area of entrepreneurship, markets and value chains that different development organizations were already undertaking or were planning. It avoided each organization starting its own initiative with its own partners, instead opening participation to a larger group, promoting exchange and saving costs.

Haricot beans, soybeans and linseed

Improving market arrangements: The Burka Gudina Cooperative

Location:	Kerenso Kubie, Shalla woreda, West Arsi zone, Oromia state
Founded:	2004
Members:	899 (109 women)
Product:	Haricot beans
Supported by:	CDI (Centre for Development Initiatives) and ICCO
Business contest:	Funding strategy prize ✦

A farmers' cooperative that buys and sells grain, sells fertilizer and improved seed to its members, and owns a vehicle that offers a public transport service.

The members of the Burka Gudina cooperative were frustrated: local traders would offer only ETB 150 per 100 kg bag for their haricot beans, even though the same items would sell in Addis Ababa for more than twice that (ETB 380) after passing through the hands of several intermediate traders. This was a problem for neighbouring cooperatives as well.

Through the Learning Alliance, Burka Gudina learned how to seek alternative markets for a high-value product such as haricot beans. They identified ACOS Ethiopia, a major exporter of haricot beans, approached them and negotiated a deal to supply an initial 300 tonnes of haricot as well as 600 tonnes of maize. To meet this demand, Burka Gudina made agreements with four other cooperatives. To facilitate an increase of volume, ACOS agreed to provide the farmers with high-quality seed. In 2008, these arrangements resulted in a good yield of 2.6 tons per ha. The farmers brought the beans to Nazareth where the exporter bought 247 tons but rejected 24 tons because of high moisture content caused by the rains at harvest time. The rejected haricots were sold to other traders at a lower price.

This setback made the five cooperatives hesitant to purchase more haricots and maize from their members. But at the same time they also felt proud that they could handle the logistics and secure good prices for their members. The cooperatives, the exporter and CDI discussed how to further improve the performance for the next season. The five farmers' organizations committed themselves to maintain good quality and proper handling of the product. ACOS agreed to support them during the harvest and to take care of storing the beans. It also agreed to provide seeds and sacks, as well as reliable market information. CDI gave refresher training on product quality and facilitated coordination and communication between the cooperatives and the exporter.

The cooperatives have also found a second major customer, the World Food Programme, and further high-volume sales are in prospect. One member, Mamma Tefo, says that he built a house from his haricot profits. *"I used to live in a small hut with a thatched roof"*, he says. *"Now I am living in a house made of corrugated iron."*

From soybeans to milk: Tulu Ifa Farmers' Marketing Organization

Location:	Busa, Tiro Afeta woreda, Jimma zone, Oromia state
Founded:	2000
Members:	147 members (25 women)
Product:	Soybean
Supported by:	Facilitators for Change (FC) and ICCO

A cooperative that markets its members' soybeans

Cow's milk is not readily available in the city of Jimma, and Orthodox Christians are expected to abstain from animal products for some 200 days a year. Two good reasons for local farmers to grow soybeans, which can be turned into a nutritious milk substitute. But the members of the Tulu Ifa Farmers' Marketing Organization, which markets soybean, were not able to take advantage of this opportunity. It lacked a clear plan and did not know how to identify potential buyers or promote its product. It desperately needed working capital but did not know how to get a loan.

Tulu Ifa learned how to tackle these things through the Learning Alliance. Its partner, Facilitators for Change, held an exhibition about soybeans, and distributed a booklet on

processing the crop. It developed ties with the Jimma Agricultural Research Centre to get technical support. It also helped secure a contractual agreement with a local processor interested in soymilk. The contract specified a higher price than what was offered by the market, covering costs for collection and grading by the farmers' organization. This price is expected to stimulate production and promote soybean as crop to rotate with maize.

In June 2009 Tulu Ifa obtained a loan of ETB 62,000 from the Harbu Micro Finance Institution. That enabled it to buy 10 tonnes of soybeans from its members and to sell it to the milk processor. This one transaction generated a profit of ETB 11,900.

Tulu Ifa's business plan outlines its dream to sell soybean by-products to cattle-fattening farms, increase its capital base by 5% a year, and target new clients in Addis Ababa. Tulu Ifa aims to increase the number of women members by waiving or delaying their payment of membership fees.

Bringing the market to the village:
Tullu Farmers' Marketing Organization

Location:	Gimbi, Tokke Kuttaye woreda, West Shoa zone, Oromia state
Founded:	2003
Members:	926 members (49 women)
Product:	Linseed
Supported by:	Ethiopian Rural Self Help Association (ERSHA), and ICCO

A farmers' organization that sells linseed to an oil processor.

It is 24 km from Gimbi to the market in the town of Guder. That is a long way driving a donkey laden with your grain. It is even longer if you are a woman carrying a 50 kg sack – for the local culture prohibits men from carrying heavy loads. And many of the farmers in Gimbi cannot afford to hire a donkey to take their produce to market. But it is the men, not their wives, who are said to spend the proceeds of the sale.

What to do if you have to go so far to the market? The answer, the members of the Tullu Farmers' Marketing Organization have found, is to bring the market to you.

When the local farmers founded the Tullu organization in 2003, they had four main problems: distance to the market, low prices set by a few brokers and traders, low profits, and including a range of commodities in the business. Through the Learning Alliance, the farmers have begun to solve all four.

The farmers concluded that they should focus on a single crop. They chose linseed, which grows well in the area, requires few inputs, and is in high demand. The Learning Alliance helped them to get to meet buyers' associations. Tullu struck a deal with an oil-processing factory which needs 20,000 tons of linseed each season. Under the agreement, the Tullu farmers can supply 3,000 tons – their whole output. In addition, Tullu can source an additional 5,000 tons from fellow farmers' organizations. There is still enough room for more production, and improved seeds from a nearby agricultural research station are expected to boost yields. Tullu has invested in accurate scales: previously, it was losing as much as 5 kg per bag because of incorrect measurements. Now members can be sure they are not losing out.

The women are spared from having to carry heavy loads to market. They play an important role in the organization, and about one-third of Tullu's management team are women.

5 Lessons

This chapter draws lessons from the Learning Alliance experience. The sections below correspond to the four preceding chapters.

Context (Chapter 1)

A combination of factors made the Learning Alliance a useful initiative to promote marketing and entrepreneurship among farmers in Ethiopia:

- Agriculture is a large and vital part of Ethiopia's economy, and a shift to the market economy poses many challenges for farmers. A lack of marketing and business skills is a major impediment to improving livelihoods of rural people.

- The Learning Alliance fits well with the government's, NGOs' and donors' goals of promoting rural development by strengthening the capacity and market orientation of farmers' organizations.

- Members of the Dutch Agri-ProFocus partnership active in Ethiopia found each other in a shared interest and were willing to pool resources to create a network of farmers' organizations, local NGOs and development organizations enabling them to experiment, learn from and support one another.

- Ethiopian partners were eager to learn more about value chains. The main NGOs working on rural development in the country participated in the Alliance. A representative group of farmers' organizations took part in the initiative.

Recommendations

- In Ethiopia, Learning Alliances should cover **smaller geographical areas** to reduce the difficulties of language and cost of travelling long distances. Apart from creating greater synergy among the participants, this would enable more women and local entrepreneurs to participate. It would also make it is easy for local NGOs to replicate the Learning Alliance initiative in their areas.

- Further develop the Learning Alliance approach to widen the learning among farmers' organizations, NGOs and development partners with **private sector players**. Businesses are key actors in the value chain and the Alliance needs to be attractive to motivate them to participate. Experiment with new practices that appeal to private sector players: not typically the NGO activities such as workshops but short meetings, diner debates, factory visits etc.

- Consider using the Learning Alliance approach to address skill development and learning in **other issues** such as natural resource management, education, and health.

The Learning Alliance approach (Chapter 2)

The Learning Alliance approach consisted of a cycle of initial workshops, assignments, coaching and exchange workshops.

Workshops

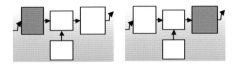

The workshops were a vital part of the Learning Alliance process: they enabled the participants to meet and share ideas, learn new concepts and skills, design and refine assignments, and check on progress. They were held in different locations to enable participants to learn about different farming conditions. Ideally, the same participants should have attended each workshop to ensure continuity and develop their skills, but in fact, different farmers attended each time. From a different angle, this could also be seen as positive: more farmers were able to get familiar with how the Learning Alliance organized its workshops. Few women farmers attended, reflecting the small number of women in leadership positions and the difficulty they face in travelling long distances to attend such events. It was also difficult to attract representatives of the private sector to attend, though they did attend coaching sessions where they could meet with farmers and negotiate with them.

The design of the workshops was important. A variety of activities, including plenaries, small group sessions, panels, field visits, games, story-telling, farmer presentations, speed-dating and energizers, helped maintain interest and energy levels. The number and length of plenary sessions had to be limited because all what was said was translated into Amharic or English; this slowed down the pace of the workshops, making them less dynamic.

Recommendations on workshops

- Plan the **first workshop** carefully: it is key for generating commitment in the process and defining what to do. Use it to organize support for the learning activities by involving senior managers of the organizations involved.

- Encourage the farmers' organizations to send the **same representatives** to each workshop, and to have **women farmers** participate.

- Actively approach **entrepreneurs** to provoke their interest in what the Alliance does and invite them to key workshop sessions (since it is not likely they will attend the whole workshop). Moreover, put a major effort in involving them in the coaching activities.

- Reduce plenary sessions and organize small group work in the **farmers' languages** (field visits, group discussions, games etc.).

- Introduce **field visits** to break the routine and to connect to follow-up assignments.

- Design the workshops in such a way that participants understand and prepare for **assignments** once they go home. Include a debriefing on the assignments in the next workshop.

- Hold workshops in **different locations** to vary travel time for participants and to expose them to new places during field visits.

- Ensure the **venue** is appropriate, with proper sound system, nice atmosphere, and enough space for break-out groups and group work. Do not save on the quality of food and drinks.

- **Combine** exchange and initial workshops to save on costs. Introducing a new topic will also help you to gain momentum and refresh energies of the participants.

Assignments

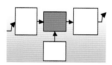

The assignments were developed during the workshops and were tailored to the participants' situation and needs. They guided the farmers' organizations through a step in the process of exploring and developing their markets and value chains. They required the farmers' organizations to do market research, talk to traders and banks, develop a business plan, and so on.

Three general problems arose in the assignments:

- **Writing**. Most of the writing and reporting was done by the NGOs rather than the farmers' organizations, especially during the first steps of the Alliance. The farmers participated in discussions, but found it difficult to fill in forms or write reports.

- **Deadlines**. Most participants had problems meeting the deadlines. They waited for the coaching before starting the assignments. This meant that most coaching time was spent on the assignment's paperwork, leaving less time for analysing results or tailor-made advice. In some cases, the coaches used part of the exchange workshops to finalize the assignment.

- **Different speeds**. In Step 4, it became evident that the farmers' organizations and their NGOs had progressed at different speeds. For the assignment in Step 5, it was decided to divide the organizations into three groups, each with assignments to suit their current situation.

Recommendations on assignments

- The assignments need to be relevant: adapt them to match **the needs and conditions** of the participants (reflecting farmers' realities).

- Instead of requiring written reports, use the first morning of the exchange workshop to **discuss the results** of the previous assignment. Allow for presenting the results in different ways such as a poster presentation or story telling.

- Keep reporting by farmers simple: ask them to make **oral presentations** to complement the written documents, and use information from the coaching sessions for additional insights on the progress made.

- Treat the assignments as a **tool**, not as a goal in themselves.

- Make sure that the **NGO** is not doing all the work for the assignment: it is a joint effort.

Coaching

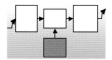

For the farmers' organizations and their NGO partners, the coaching visits were the most visible part of the Learning Alliance process. Because the coaches visited each location, more members could take part: coaching sessions had between three and 17 participants. It was also easier for women members, local business partners and government officials to participate. The sessions enabled the coaches to focus on the specific situation and needs of each farmers' organization.

Among the major issues arising in the coaching sessions were:

- **Language**. Some of the coaches could not speak the local language, so coaches worked in pairs to ensure that they had the right combination of language and subject skills.

- **Distance**. It proved impossible for the coaches to visit the most distant organizations in each step. That meant they had to be coached in Addis Ababa or by telephone.

- **Subject area**. The coaches lacked the specific knowledge and skills to coach the farmer organizations on financial issues. For this reason, a finance specialist was hired to visit all 18 farmers' organizations and assist them with the assignment. This same person did a second round of coaching to help them prepare their business plans.

- **Time available**. Coaching needs enough time to do a proper job. Sometimes the coaching sessions pushed for the completion of assignments instead of supporting the value chain empowerment process.

- **Coaching skills**. Coaches require special skills: transparency, empathy, good listening skills, and authenticity. They must build a relationship of trust with their clients. Learning these skills takes time.

Recommendations on coaching

- Plan sufficient **time and funding** for coaching. Coaching is an essential link between the workshops and it allows for tailor-made advice suiting the participants' situation and experiences.

- Allow enough time and effort on both sides to develop a relationship of **trust** and openness.

- In coaching, go **beyond the immediate assignment**, looking into other critical factors of the farmers' organization.

- **Train coaches** to prepare them for the job. Create a space where they can exchange experiences to learn from each other.

Steps in the Learning Alliance cycle (Chapter 3)

The Learning Alliance followed six steps, beginning with mapping the present chain relations, and ending with presenting a business plan. From a value chain perspective, this is a logical order for teaching an enterprise development process. The number of steps might be increased or decreased depending on the situation and needs of the farmers' groups. Likewise, the content of each step can be adjusted to best fit the context.

The step most discussed was the business plan contest. At first, there was some resistance to the idea of a competition. The learning-by-doing principle involved sharing among the farmers' organizations, and now the farmers became competitors for the same funds. NGOs did not like to separate 'winners' from the rest. But the farmers were very motivated to participate in the contest and were eager to hear the jury's criteria. There was a lot of energy in this final phase.

Why stop with the business plan? It might have been better to continue the Learning Alliance to build on the plans and help the farmers' organizations put them into practice, rather than leaving them and their supporting NGOs to do so alone. One development organization organized a meeting with the NGOs and farmers' organizations they are supporting, but others provided none or little guidance to the implementation of the business plans.

Going through the different steps it was necessary to monitor both the learning process as a whole and the progress of each farmers' organization. Monitoring methods included evaluation sessions in each workshop, as well as coaches checking on the progress made in members' participation, business-related knowledge, commercial relationships and overall business behaviour.

Recommendations on the steps

- Follow the farmers **after the business plans** have been developed, accompany the groups as they implement their plans.

- A **business contest** with prize money is very motivating for participants. But allow time to discuss the idea of a contest, and make sure the whole process is transparent for all participants and make sure that especially the award ceremony fully respects those that are not among the winners.

- Monitor both the overall learning process and the progress of each farmers' organization. Accept **different speeds of learning** and use coaching for specific support.

Results of the Learning Alliance (Chapter 4)

All three types of organizations involved in the Learning Alliance changed as a result of their participation in the Alliance. They learned new skills in marketing, enterprise and value chain development, planning and training; they gained insights into unfamiliar fields, and they built relationships with traders, buyers, service providers and development organizations. They learned that others face similar problems and together sought solutions to these problems.

In the initial planning of the Learning Alliance, one objective was "to create an apex body of farmers' organizations". This objective was not accomplished. On the contrary, the business contest led to a feeling of competition. Still, in two of the winning business plans, farmers' organizations proposed joint action: they planned to achieve better market prices by bulking their products with those of neighbouring groups.

Throughout the process, successful learning depended on the drive that farmers' organizations had. Some had a clear perspective and were able to learn and build their capacities easily. Others seemed to have the internal capacity in place, but lacked the initiative and motivation to make a difference. As the process progressed, the farmers became more confident in their relationship with their support NGOs, and started to learn alongside the NGO field staff. Several of the NGOs, in turn, realized they needed more business skills, and requested further training (some of this was provided by SNV and ICCO). An important factor in the Learning Alliance's success was that the eight development partners provided a solid core of staff who shared a commitment from start till finish.

Although the coaching visits and workshops generated insights in the results being achieved by the Learning Alliance, more attention could have been given to monitor the changes at household level. This is not an easy task since it will always be difficult to link the changes as a direct result of the Learning Alliance: prices changes, other support programmes, new policies etc. will also influence the farmers. Yet, this does not mean no effort should be made to obtain figures on data such as the membership of farmer organizations, turnover, profit, income etc. If this is not integrated right at the start of the initiative, it will most likely be pushed aside by urgent operational and organizational concerns popping up while running the Alliance. For in-depth insight in the impact of the initiative ask participants at the end of the process to list the most important change they experienced as a result of the Learning Alliance. Writing stories about the main thing they learned also generated valuable information on the impact of the Alliance on people's lives.

Recommendations on results

- Make sure that the Learning Alliance remains relevant for its participants by regularly sensing whether the **most relevant issues** are being covered. Be critical whether the farmers' organizations are able to maintain the drive and develop the capacities needed to improve their performance.

- Encourage farmers to **share and organize with other groups** when this makes economic sense. Help build trust with neighbouring groups of farmers.

- Keep interested **non-participants** within the participating organizations informed to avoid creating a closed inner circle of committed staff.

- Be aware that the role of NGOs and consultants is **to guide** the development of the business plan, and not to write it.

- Consider web tools such as email groups and wikis to enable communication among development partners and NGO head offices. Make sure that information is also channelled to field offices and farmers' organizations. Think of alternative ways of communicating with those farmer organisations that do **not have access to internet**.

- Design a practical way of **monitoring** progress right at the start of the process. Before you know, you will be too busy with running the Alliance. At the final workshop ask participants to mention the main change they experienced as a result of the Alliance. Urge them to tell **stories** on what they learned and writing these down with the help of journalist is a precious source of information too.

How much did the Learning Alliance cost?

The central budget of the Learning Alliance was €222,500. ICCO and Agriterra each contributed €80,000, and Cordaid €62,500. Financial management was coordinated between by ICCO and Agri-ProFocus.

The budget covered the cost of workshops, travel and participants' accommodation. It also covered 50% of the support provided by KIT, the other half was financed by KIT itself. It included the costs relating to coaching, mainly travel cost, communication and hiring local consultants. It also covered translation of documents into Amharic and English, travel by the contest jury, documentation, and communication. Finally, there was the prize money for the business plan contest (in total €75,000).

Each development partner contributed staff time and covered the costs for their staff travelling to Ethiopia and to participate in the workshops. The financial contributions and the provision of staff time were formally anchored in a memorandum of understanding signed by all development partners.

The support team in Ethiopia (involving FFARM, ICCO-Ethiopia, SNV-Ethiopia and IIRR-Ethiopia) invested about 625 working days over the 3 years the Alliance was operational. The five development partners in the Netherlands invested an additional 225 working days. Most staff input came from KIT and Agri-ProFocus.

The Learning Alliance had on average 68 participants in each workshop. A typical coaching session was attended by 8-10 farmers, making some 162 participants in all for each round of coaching. The total number of farmers participating in the Learning Alliance was almost 5,400.

Table 1 summarizes the operational costs and staff time spent in the Learning Alliance, including a calculation on the cost per participant. Although without having a clear benchmark, the people involved considered the Alliance to be a good investment considering the results obtained and acknowledge that it was a first time experiment.

Recommendations on costs

- Costs of organizing a Learning Alliance always need to be compared with **alternatives** that generate a similar result in terms of skill development, increased income, and empowerment of farmers.

- Include from the start a strategy of **up-scaling** where participating NGOs and farmer organizations will replicate the approach with other NGOs and farmers in other areas.

- An obvious option to reduce the funding costs is to gear the business contest towards real-life **investors**. In this option banks and other financial institutions replace the independent jury and bring in investment capital instead of prize money.

- One option is to focus on a **smaller geographic area**, which brings down the cost of transport and stay of both workshops and coaching.

- One possibility to increase outreach is to train a number of participants to play the **role of coaches** and have a central team supporting them ("coach the coaches").

Table 1.   Operational costs of the Learning Alliance

Activities	€ 147,500
Staff time	850 working days (625 local)
Prize money	€ 75,000
Total (without staff time)	**€ 222,500**
Number of participating farmers	5400
Cost per participant (total budget)	€ 41
Cost per participant (excluding prize money)	€ 27

Comparing the Learning Alliance with a standard series of training workshops

The Learning Alliance described in this book is quite different from running "yet another" series of training events, considering the following aspects:

- Just as important as the workshops were the **assignment** and **coaching** sessions.

- Central in the design of the Alliance was **a sequence of steps** which needed to be followed, ending in a business plan contest.

- The themes covered in the steps were chosen in direct consultation with the participating farmer organizations and NGOs, responding to their **needs and interests**. While the Learning Alliance progressed, regular checks took place where participants were asked if the themes were still relevant and top priority.

- Lectures and plenary sessions were far less important **training tools** than field visits, games, group work, market place, story telling etc. and proved to be much more dynamic and effective.

- **Joint skills development** through "learning by doing" and through the interaction of a mix of private sector, NGO, government, donor and research organizations was essential to the approach.

- Departing from a **framework** of chain empowerment through which farmers develop strategies to strengthen their position in the chain.

This book has offered insights in organizing a Learning Alliance to support farmer entrepreneurship and their empowerment in value chains which might be of use in rural development. The authors would be interested to learn of similar initiatives in Ethiopia or elsewhere. Please contact us at the e-mail addresses on page 11.

Honey and incense

Incense and gum no longer a taboo:
Goro Roba Marketing Cooperative

Location: Erdar, Dhas woreda, Borana zone, Oromia state
Founded: 2007
Members: 48 members (21 women)
Product: Incense, gum
Supported by: Action for Development (AFD), ICCO and Cordaid
Business contest: Gender prize (joint winner) ✦

A cooperative of pastoralists who tap resins from trees.

For the pastoralists of Dhas woreda, livestock means wealth. They used to sneer at people who tapped the area's trees for resin and incense: such people were regarded as the poorest of the poor. Some were even hounded out of the community because tapping trees was considered a taboo.

That is now changing, thanks to the Goro Roba Marketing Cooperative. Established in 2007 with 38 members, this cooperative used a seed fund of ETB 30,000 from Action for Development to acquire equipment to harvest and purify the resin. Members learned how to manage and plan a business, calculate costs, save money, and improve the quality and quantity of the gum they produce.

Goro Roba buys incense and gum from its members at ETB 7/kg, and sells it in bulk at ETB 9/kg. Earnings have jumped and profits are rising every year. From being among the poorest people in the area, members are now among the better-off. The cooperative helps poorer members by building houses, buying them goats and paying for medical expenses. As the members' confidence has increased, so too has acceptance by their neighbours, and the Goro Roba has grown as new members have joined. In 2010 it planned to sell 13.4 tonnes of incense and 3.2 tonnes of gum in the towns of Yabello and Moyale, where demand and prices are higher than from local traders.

Women gain confidence: Sochi Gudina Marketing Cooperative

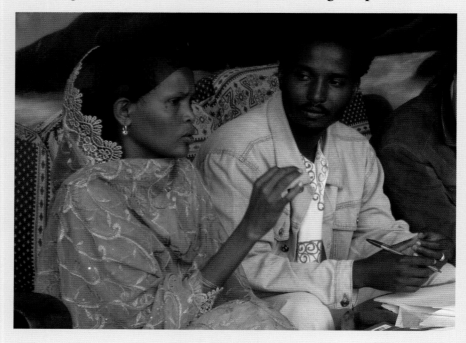

Location:	Wachile, Arero woreda, Borana zone, Oromia state
Founded:	2007
Members:	52 (28 women)
Product:	Incense
Supported by:	Action for Development (AFD), ICCO, and Cordaid
Business contest:	Gender prize (joint winner) +

A cooperative of pastoralists who tap resins from trees.

Women play a big role in the Sochi Gudina Marketing Cooperative. In Sochi Gudina, women account for more than half the cooperative's members, and the purchasing manager, auditor and cashier are all women.

It was not always like that. Financial transactions are normally handled by men in Arero woreda, so women were at first not allowed to do any banking. But this has changed, in part because of the training the members have received through the Learning Alliance. The women members are now regarded as fully trustworthy, especially when it comes to money. They have been elected to key posts in the cooperative. Their confidence has improved along with their living standards.

Sochi Gudina specializes in marketing incense and gum produced by its members. It sells these products to merchants in Yabello and Moyale, who offer higher prices than local traders. But Sochi Gudina is exploring even better market options in Addis Ababa and elsewhere. It has sent samples of its produce to ten large potential customers.

In 2007, the cooperative bought 3 tons of gum and incense at an average price of ETB 3.50/kg, and sold it for an average of ETB 4.50/kg. It has since improved its product quality with techniques learned from training organized by Action for Development. It currently purchases gum and incense at ETB 7.75 per kg and sells these for ETB 8.00/kg. The higher prices stimulate the members to continue producing high quality. The cooperative expects to meet its plan to sell 52.5 tons of incense and 2 tons of gum a year.

As sweet as honey: Wollela Multipurpose Cooperative

Location: Adama woreda, East Shoa zone, Oromia state
Founded: 2003
Members: 127 (47 women)
Product: Honey
Supported by: East Shoa Beekeepers Association (ESBA), and SNV
Business contest: Capacity building prize +

A multi-purpose cooperative that refines and sells honey and beeswax.

Much of the honey produced in Ethiopia is turned into tej, a spiced alcoholic beverage regarded as the national drink. Beeswax, made from the honeycombs, is used to make candles that light thousands of churches around the country.

So beekeeping might seem a sweet business to be in. But the Wollela cooperative found that its business was going sour. It managed to market 3 tons of honey and a ton of beeswax a month, but was reluctant to buy and sell more: lacking information about the level of demand, it was afraid of losing money.

The Learning Alliance's assignments, coaching, visits and workshops have set the cooperative buzzing. It improved its management, planning and marketing, and has created new jobs in processing and selling honey. It has trained its members how to improve the quality of the honey and wax they supply to the cooperative. It has discovered that its potential market is larger than it thought, and has been able to expand its business. It now buys as much as 18 tons of honey and 7 tons of wax a month, and has added four shops to the one it already owned.

Wollela sees wax as a promising area for further expansion. One kilogram of purified wax fetches ETB 45, compared to just ETB 7 for a kilogram of unpurified honey. Demand for wax is high: apart from candles, it is used in cosmetics, medicine, food packaging and as a foundation for honeycombs in new hives.

Partnering with a private company: Agama Forest User Group

Location: Bito, Gimbo woreda, Kaffa zone, SNNPR state
Founded: 2002
Members: 198 members (96 women)
Product: Honey
Supported by: Apinec SNV, and Cordaid
Business contest: Third prize ✳

An organization of forest users that collaborates with a private company to produce and sell honey.

A forest is full of trees, and trees are made of wood: a tempting source of timber, firewood and money. So is it a good idea to chop the forest down in search of a quick birr?

No, according to the Agama Forest User Group, a group of about 200 farmers who have agreed to protect the 1,241 ha of forest surrounding their village. They rely on the forest for their living. So instead of axes and chainsaws, they are using hives and buckets to collect honey, a form of riches that the forest can produce on a sustainable basis.

Founded in 2002, Agama used its membership of the Learning Alliance as a springboard to learn new management and production skills, and to improve its marketing. It allied with Apinec, a honey processor and beeswax producer. Apinec has its own hives but also sources from outgrowers. The Agama group supplies Apinec with raw or semi-processed honey and wax; in return, Apinec provides it with training and with interest-free loans that it can use to buy these products from its members. Both sides stand to gain: Apinec gets a reliable supply of materials, while the Agama group gets support, loans, and a dependable customer.

The Learning Alliance has helped the Agama group improve its financial records, better plan its activities, and increase its efficiency. The loans from Apinec have enabled the group to buy ETB 85,000 worth of honey, compared to just ETB 15,000 three years before. It has also started using equipment to process its honey and improve its quality.

Prices have gone up as a result. One member of the group, Issa Mohammed, says that his income has risen significantly. He used to sell a kilogram of crude honey for only ETB 15, and a kilo of wax at ETB 25. After refining, his honey now fetches ETB 24 a kilogram, while wax has doubled in price. He built a new house and bought modern beehives with the proceeds.

Resources

Ethiopian Government Portal, no date.
www.ethiopia.gov.et/English

KIT, Faida MaLi and IIRR. 2006. *Chain empowerment: Supporting African farmers to develop markets.* Royal Tropical Institute, Amsterdam, Faida Market Link, Arusha, and International Institute of Rural Reconstruction, Nairobi. http://www.kit.nl/net/KIT_Publicaties_output/showfile.aspx?e=1647

KIT and IIRR. 2008. *Trading up: Building cooperation between farmers and traders in Africa.* Royal Tropical Institute, Amsterdam, and International Institute of Rural Reconstruction, Nairobi. http://www.kitpublishers.nl/net/KIT_Publicaties_output/showfile.aspx?e=1441

KIT and IIRR, 2010. *Value Chain Finance: Beyond microfinance for rural entrepreneurs.* Royal Tropical Institute, Amsterdam and International Institute of Rural Reconstruction, Nairobi. http://www.kitpublishers.nl/net/KIT_Publicaties_output/showfile.aspx?e=1610

Lundy, M., M.V. Gottret and J. Ashby. 2005. Learning alliances: An approach for building multi-stakeholder innovation systems, *ILAC Brief* 8, August 2005. Institutional Learning and Change Initiative (ILAC). http://www.cgiar-ilac.org/files/publications/briefs/ILAC_Brief08_alliances.pdf

Lundy, M. 2006. Change through shared learning. *LEISA Magazine* 22.3, Sep 2006. pp. 18–19. Leusden, Netherlands. http://www.agriculturesnetwork.org/magazines/global/building-knowledge/change-through-shared-learning

Lundy, M. and M.V. Gottret, 2007. Learning alliances: Building multi-stakeholder innovation systems in agro-enterprise development. In: S. Smits, P. Moriarity and C. Sijbesma (eds). *Learning alliances: Scaling up innovations in water, sanitation and hygiene.* International Water and Sanitation Centre (IRC), technical paper series 47, pp. 37–57. Delft, Netherlands. http://www.irc.nl/page/35887

MoFED, 2010. *Growth and Transformation Plan (GTP) 2010/11 – 2014/15,* Ministry of Finance and Economic Development, Federal Democratic Republic of Ethiopia. http://www.mofed.gov.et/English/Resources/Documents/GTP%20English2.pdf

UNdata. no date. *Country profile Ethiopia.* United Nations Statistics Division (UNSD). http://data.un.org/CountryProfile.aspx?crName=Ethiopia

Vorley, B., A. Fearne and D. Ray (eds). 2007. Regoverning markets: A place for small-scale producers in modern agrifood chains? IIED, Gower Sustainable Food Chains Series.

Annex 1. The Learning Alliance partners

Main product	Name of farmers' organization	Total members (women members)	Location (kebele, woreda, zone, state)	Local NGO	Development organization
Teff (page 22)					
Teff	Edero Cooperative	743 (182)	Denbi Gerarge, Ennesaro, North Shoa, Amhara	Ethiopian Orthodox Church – Development and Inter Church Aid Commision	ICCO
Teff	Ifabari and 3 other FMOs	372 (71)	Borecho, Dendii, West Shoa, Oromia	HUNDEE Oromo Grassroots Development Initiative	ICCO
Teff	Abdi Boru Farmers' Marketing Association	83 (30)	Bacho, South West Shoa, Oromia	Oromo Self-Reliance Association	ICCO
Teff	Gole Roge and 6 other FMOs	107 (30)	Nanno Garbel, South West Shoa, Oromia	Facilitators for Change	ICCO
Wheat and maize (page 37)					
Maize	Lalisa Walgayi Karro Gayib Cooperative	410 (73)	Sayo, Dembi Dollo, Kellem Wollega, Oromia	Nekemte Catholic Secretariat	Cordaid
Wheat	Alabedas Farmers' Marketing Organization and 5 other FMOs	628 (187)	Chelanko, Jelduu, West Shoa, Oromia	HUNDEE Oromo Grassroots Development Initiative	ICCO
Wheat	Meja Gero Farmers' Organization	55 (15)	Meja Gero, Arsi Negele, East Arsi, Oromia	African Development Aid Association	ICCO
Wheat	Dedie Farmers' Cooperative	253 (84)	Durame, Kembata Tembaro, SNNPR	International Institute of Rural Reconstruction	ICCO

Dairy and coffee (page 65)				
Milk	Biruh Tesfah Dairy Producers' Cooperative	Addis Alem, Ejera, West Shoa, Oromia	Self Help Africa	ICCO
Milk	Gelgel Dairy Producers' Cooperative	Holeta, Walmara, West Shoa, Oromia	Self Help Africa	ICCO
Coffee	Dimbira Coffee Farmers' Cooperative	Dimbira, Chenna, Kaffa, SNNPR	Jima Bonga Catholic Secretariat	Cordaid
Haricot beans, soybean and linseed (page 77)				
Haricot beans	Burka Gudina and 4 other cooperatives	Kerenso Kubie, Shalla, West Arsi zone, Oromia	Center for Development Initiatives	ICCO
Soybean	Tulu Ifa Farmers' Marketing Organization	Busa, Tiro Afeta, Jimma, Oromia	Facilitators for Change	ICCO
Linseed	Tullu Farmers' Marketing Organization and 5 other FMOs	Gimbi, Tokke Kuttaye, West Shoa, Oromia	Ethiopian Rural Self Help Association	ICCO
Honey and incense (page 93)				
Incense and gum	Goro Roba Marketing Cooperative	Erdar, Dhas, Borana, Oromia	Action for Development	ICCO/ Cordaid
Incense and gum	Sochi Gudina Marketing Cooperative	Wachile, Arero, Borana, Oromia	Action for Development	ICCO/ Cordaid
Honey	Wollela Multipurpose Cooperative	Adama, East Shoa, Oromia	East Shoa Beekeepers Association	SNV
Honey	Agama Forest User Group	Bito, Gimbo, Kaffa, SNNPR	Apinec Agro-Industry plc	SNV Cordaid
Total	**18**		14	5

Value in "Milk" rows: 60 (10), 41 (3); Coffee: 243 (84); Haricot beans: 899 (109); Soybean: 147 (25); Linseed: 926 (49); Incense and gum: 48 (21); Incense and gum: 52 (28); Honey: 127 (47); Honey: 198 (96); Total: 5,392 (1,144)

Annex 2. Development organizations in the Learning Alliance

Organization	Purpose	Additional information	Role in Learning Alliance
Agri-ProFocus	Creating joint action and learning networks for farmer entrepreneurship	www.agri-profocus.nl apf-ethiopia.ning.com	Coordination
Agriterra	Working with rural people who are truly dedicated to eradicate poverty by getting organized	www.agriterra.org	Funding
Cordaid Catholic Organisation for Relief and Development Aid	Combining experience and expertise in emergency aid and structural poverty eradication, always working with partners organizations	www.cordaid.nl	Funding
FFARM Facilitating Farmers' Access to Remunerative Markets	Business development services to support organizations in increasing productivity and improving access to markets		Coaching
ICCO Interchurch Organisation for Development Cooperation	Giving financial support and advice to local organizations and networks working for better access to basic facilities, initiating sustainable economical development and enhancing peace and democracy	www.icco.nl	Coaching, funding
IIRR International Institute of Rural Reconstruction	Building the capacity of the poor and their organizations to overcome poverty so that they can attain justice, equity and peace	www.iirr.org	Coaching, workshop facilitation
KIT Royal Tropical Institute	Contribute through knowledge and expertise to sustainable development, poverty alleviation and cultural preservation and exchange	www.kit.nl	Technical expertise
SNV Netherlands Development Organisation	Alleviate poverty by enabling lowest incomes to be part of social and economic networks and so increase their income and employment opportunities	www.snvworld.org	Coaching

Annex 3. Prize winners of the business plan contest

Prizes	Commodity	Winner (support NGO)	Focus during the Learning Alliance	Highlights from the business plan	Income projection (gross profit first year)
First prize * (€14,000)	Teff	Ifabari and 3 FMOs (HUNDEE)	Finance (savings group, access to credit) Inputs (improved teff seed) Market links (mapping of processors)	Upscaling of teff trading by bulking more volume with 4 other farmers' organizations Improving quality throughout the chain, by grading 2 qualities, dedicated sales to 3 traders, relating to research, NGO, cooperative desk for chain support	ETB 147,000 from sale of 293 tons (margin ETB 5/ton)
Second prize * (€12,000)	Teff	Gole Roge and 6 FMOs (FC)	Mapping the chain: identified exporter as buyer and access to quality seed Business planning of bulking product	Upscaling the trade, buying from 6 FMOs and selling in bulk to 2 dedicated clients (exporter) Plan to start small flour mill for local clients and members' home consumption	ETB 301,000 from sale of 282 tons (margin ETB 11/ton)
Third prize * (€10,000)	Honey	Agama Forest User Group (APINEC)	Farmers already have APINEC as buyer Strengthening actors: quality problems tackled by all parties (exporter, NGO and farmers' organizations)	Quality: Apinec support aimed at export quality assurance Business support for quality improvements and improved hives	ETB 214,000 from sale of 8,239 kg honey, 4,206 kg wax and 1,402 litres of *berth* (local drink) (margin ETB 104/beehive)
Special prizes					
Capacity development + (€6,000)	Honey	Wollela Co-op (East Shoa Beekeepers Association)	Rethinking marketing strategy, besides honey also wax Strengthening coop by training members	Plan to purify and sell wax in addition to honey Plan to acquire vehicle for transport	Not mentioned in the business plan

Special prizes					
Gender + (€3,000) Shared prize	Incense, gum	Goro Roba Co-op (Action for Development)	Strengthening actors: profits led to changed perceptions of gum collection and role of women. Finding new market opportunities for improved quality, bypassing middlemen	Contact other farmers' organizations for bulking of product. Contact bigger traders for better prices	ETB 97,000 from sale of 134 sacks of incense and 32 sacks of gum
Gender + (€3,000) Shared prize	Incense, gum	Sochi Gudina Co-op (Action for Development)	Strengthening actors: profits led to changed perceptions of gum collection and role of women. Finding new market opportunities for improved quality, bypassing middlemen	Contact other farmers' organizations for bulking of product. Contact bigger traders for better prices	ETB 32,000 from sale of 525 sacks of incense and 20 sacks of gum
Funding strategy + (€6,000)	Haricot beans	Burka Gudina and 4 co-ops (Center for Development Initiatives)	Chain mapping; the co-ops pursued new buyers for better terms and prices	The 5 co-ops agreed a contract farming arrangement with exporter, including access to improved seeds. Contacted World Food Programme as new customer. Plan to invest in threshing, winnowing and drying	ETB 394,000 from sale of 540 tons of beans (margin ETB 7/ton)
Learning strategy + (€6,000)	Maize	Lalisa Walgayi (Nekemte Catholic Secretariat)	Strengthening actors: balancing food security for members and bulking maize for sales. Chain mapping in an isolated region means extra effort to find new buyers	Expand buying from farmers; sell to bigger trader and to neighbouring regions. Buy truck for transport and flour mill for processing	ETB 147,000 from sale of 293 tons of maize (margin ETB 5/ton)
Pro-poor approach + (€6,000)	Wheat	Alabedas and 5 FMOs (HUNDEE)	Market mapping: established contacts with processors and exporter. Arranged link with research to provide quality seed	Alliance of 6 farmers' organizations to bulk and sell wheat. Build store to maintain seed quality	ETB 584,000 from sale of 432 tons of wheat (margin ETB 14/ton)

Colophon

Bulletins of the Royal Tropical Institute (KIT)

The KIT Bulletin Series deals with current themes in international development. It is a multi-disciplinary forum for scientists, policy makers, managers and development advisors in agriculture, natural resource management, health, culture, history and anthropology to present their work. These fields reflect the broad scope of KIT's activities.

KIT Development Policy & Practice

KIT Development Policy & Practice is the Royal Tropical Institute's main department for international development. Our aim is to contribute to reducing poverty and inequality in the world and to support sustainable development. We carry out research and provide advisory services and training in order to build and share knowledge on a wide range of development issues. We work in partnership with higher education, knowledge and research institutes, non-governmental and civil society organizations, and responsible private enterprises in countries around the world.

Contact information

Royal Tropical Institute (KIT)
KIT Development Policy & Practice
PO Box 95001
1090 HA Amsterdam
The Netherlands
Telephone: +31 (0)20 568 8458
Fax: +31 (0)20 568 8444
Email: development@kit.nl
Website: www.kit.nl/development

Agri-ProFocus (APF)

Agri-ProFocus (APF) is a partnership that promotes farmer entrepreneurship in developing countries. APF's founding members are Dutch NGOs, knowledge institutes and companies which promote farmer entrepreneurship. Each member has an extensive network in developing countries. Agri-ProFocus is the sum of all of these networks. By coordinating activities, exchanging information and ideas and undertaking joint action we aspire to improve existing linkages and provide a better service to farmer entrepreneurs in the South. For more information: http://www.agri-profocus.nl/.

© 2011 KIT, Amsterdam, the Netherlands

KIT Publishers

Mauritskade 63
PO Box 63
1090 HA Amsterdam
www.kitpublishers.nl
publishers@kit.nl

Coordination John Belt (KIT) and Wim Goris (Agri-ProFocus)
Editing Paul Mundy, Germany, www.mamud.com
Proof reading Rozemarijn Apotheker, Ellen Mangnus, Anna Laven, Vera Hendriks and Roel Snelders
Cover and design Ad van Helmond, Amsterdam
Photographs Petterik Wiggers (cover, page 12, 28, 44, 70 and 82), Wim Goris and John Belt
Printing Bariet bv, Ruinen

Keywords

Learning Alliance, value chain development, farmers' organizations, rural entrepreneurship, agricultural development in Ethiopia

Correct citation

Belt, J., W. Goris, S. Debela, F. Kefyalew, E. Smulders and P. Visser, 2011. *Learning and earning: How a value chain learning alliance strengthens farmer entrepreneurship in Ethiopia.* KIT Bulletin 395, KIT Publishers, Amsterdam.

ISBN 97 894 6022 179 8